AN INTRODUCTION TO THE
PROPHETS OF ISRAEL

AN INTRODUCTION TO THE
PROPHETS OF ISRAEL

Richard T. A. Murphy, OP

ST. PAUL BOOKS & MEDIA

BOSTON

Nihil Obstat
Rev. Thomas W. Buckley, S.T.D.

Imprimatur
+Bernard Cardinal Law

January 30, 1995

Library of Congress Cataloging-in-Publication Data

Murphy, Richard Thomas Aquinas, 1908-
  An introduction to the prophets of Israel / Richard T. A.
Murphy.
    p. cm.
  Includes bibliographical references.
  ISBN 0-8198-3672-9 (paper)
  1. Bible. O.T. Prophets—Introductions. I. Title.
BS1505.5.M87 1995
224'.061—dc20   95-19308
                         CIP

Design by Gregory Maria Usselmann, FSP

Printed and published by Pauline Books & Media, 50 St. Paul's
Avenue, Boston, MA 02130.

Pauline Books & Media is the publishing house of the Daughters of
St. Paul, an international congregation of women religious serving
the Church with the communications media.

1 2 3 4 5   99 98 97 96 95

Contents

List of Illustrations

Foreword

The writings of the prophets, four hundred pages in all, take up about a fourth of the Old Testament. These writings are almost three thousand years old, and it is at least a small miracle that they have survived their passage through time. Their message transcends the events that made them speak and the interval that separates them from the modern age.

Chronology and geography shed some light on the writers of these books, but there is more to them than the fact that they lived long ago in the tiny land we call Israel. What makes them so unusual is their absolute conviction that they spoke in the name of God himself. The painter Sergeant has captured something of the intensity and explosiveness of these religious-minded men.

It was not from Greece, the homeland of philosophy and art, nor from Rome, which gave the world law and order, nor from Egypt, Assyria, Babylon, or Persia, that the world learned the astonishing truth that God was not just the God of Israel; he was God of all nations and peoples. Among ancient thinkers the prophets alone perceived the profound spiritual dimension of human life, and the existence of a higher world than that of nature. Man needs more than bread to live.

This basic but revolutionary prophetic insight was in perfect harmony with the ancient Mosaic tradition. Convinced of the great importance of their timeless message, the prophets inveighed against idolatry, reminding their listeners of the importance of what they did in their daily living.

Built and sustained by power and might, the great empires of the ancient world knew only a brief, passing glory. The prophetic period in Israel was also of short duration, but the lessons the prophets taught influenced the shape of Judaism and foreshadowed the coming of Christ.

The prophetic writings obviously did not come into being overnight but were "occasional" writings, some of them representing months and even years of composition. It is not always possible to determine their precise dating, but the message itself is clear: God is interested in his world and wants to see his laws and decrees heeded and respected.

As readers of the Bible, we are often pleasantly surprised to come across phrases that have made their way into our everyday language. This Book has the capacity of startling the imagination and stirring the blood. It is part of our culture; we are constantly quoting it. Why not? Passages like the following are too good to be hidden, and we can share them on occasion with others.

Isaiah: Though your sins are like scarlet, they shall be as white as snow. Though they are red like crimson, they shall become like wool (1:18). Incline your ear, and come to me; hear, that your soul may live (55:3).

Jeremiah: My people have hewed out cisterns for themselves, broken cisterns, that can hold no water (2:13). Hear this, O...people, who have eyes, but see not, who have ears but hear not (5:21). Can the...leopard [change] his spots? (13:23)

Daniel speaks of a statue with feet of clay (2:32), of the handwriting on the wall (5:5), and of the lions' den (6:16).

Hosea, noting sadly that people perish for want of knowledge (4:6), declares that those who sow the wind will one day reap the whirlwind (8:7).

Joel provokes some serious thinking by his "Rend your hearts, not your garments" (2:13).

The prophets were men cast in a heroic mold, but they were also human like us. In the following chapters, readers will be able to gain some idea of the *who, what, where, when, and why* of the prophets. We hope that these pages, designed to introduce the prophets simply, may lead to familiarity with these admirable fellow-humans. In the process, an occasional chart or drawing will help shed some light on the world in which the prophets of Israel lived. Time spent in their company is time well spent.

Introduction

The Bible is not an answer book that solves all problems, but rather a book that enlightens, mystifies and intrigues. It proposes obscure mysteries suffused in a light so dazzling and thrilling that one hardly dares look. The Bible speaks to us of God, of his gracious plan, and of Jesus Christ.

What was this plan of God? The restoration of all things in Christ. The role of Jesus Christ was that of a Redeemer, of a Liberator from sin. This plan was only sketchily disclosed in the Bible. With time and patience, however, one comes to see that the main lines converge in the figure of Jesus of Nazareth.

Centuries ago, St. Augustine of Hippo noted how admirably the Old and New Testaments fit together. As he put it, "in the Old Testament the New lies concealed; in the New Testament the Old lies revealed."

Was Jesus spoken of in the Old Testament? Was he the long looked for Messiah? For the Church and her members, the answer is Yes. While the prophets did not always speak of the future, they sometimes did, and in the New Testament can be found what the Old promised. The answer is not mathematics. Faith is of a higher order and does justice both to history and to revelation.

Many respectable scholars have pored over the sacred text of the Bible, and have come to appreciate the perspicacity of St. Augustine. Respect for the Bible grows from contact with it, and the reason is not far to seek. The two Testaments do go together; one without the other is disjointed. One asks a question, the other answers it. Jesus spoke of the Law and the Prophets, of a time of expectation, and declared himself to be himself the answer. In his inaugural address, he said: "Think not that I have come to abolish the law and the prophets; I have come not to abolish them but to fulfil them" (Mt 5:17).

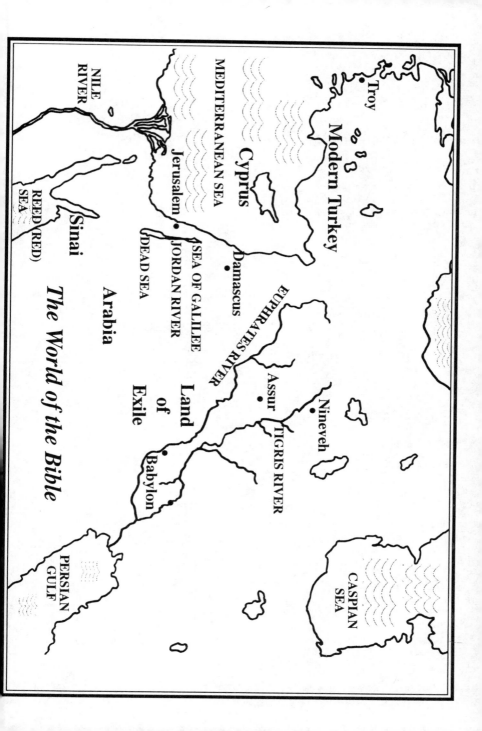

The World of the Bible

1. Introducing the Prophets

The Bible relates the fascinating story of God and his plan for the human race. It is a longish story, but it hangs together in a remarkable way. As St. Augustine put it, "In the Old Testament, the New lies concealed; in the New, the Old is revealed." Indeed, one might say (with apologies to Shakespeare) that age has not withered nor custom staled the beauty, freshness and power of the prophets and their message. The Bible is a rich mother-lode of religious thought.

Although Israel always had prophets, only a handful of them recorded what they had to say. Those who did so authored a number of *books* (actually they were *scrolls*), which would in time be gathered in a special section of the Old Testament. In Jewish tradition the prophets appear between the Historical and the Wisdom books. In Christian Bibles, the Prophetical books are at the end of the Old Testament.

Heading the list are the *major prophets*. They are so called because of their length. Isaiah has 66 chapters,

Jeremiah 52 (not counting Lamentations and Baruch), and Ezekiel 48. (Daniel, a special case, has only 12 or 14.) Another reason for calling them *major* is the fact that they bore frequent testimony to the Messiah who was to come.

Following the major prophets in the Bible are twelve who are called *minor*. They do not appear in chronological order. Thus:

Hosea	Nahum
Joel	Habakkuk
Amos	Zephaniah
Obadiah	Haggai
Jonah	Zechariah
Micah	Malachi

By arranging these books in proper chronological sequence, we can "begin at the beginning" and follow the development of the prophets' thought in an orderly fashion. In the following list, the major prophets are identified by capital letters. (Note "two" Isaiahs).

Amos (750 BC)	EZEKIEL (598-538)
Hosea (760-734)	2nd ISAIAH (586-538)
ISAIAH (736-700)	Haggai (520)
Micah (740-700)	Zechariah (520)
Zephaniah (631-609)	Malachi (450)
JEREMIAH (627-586)	Obadiah (450)
Nahum (612)	Joel
Habakkuk (605)	DANIEL (150)
	Jonah (date uncertain)

Setting for the Prophets

The prophets lived in *Israel*, a tiny strip of land on the eastern shore of the Mediterranean. To the east, beyond the Jordan, was a formidable desert; to the south, Egypt; to the north, Syria, Assyria and Babylonia, often unfriendly neighbors.

Israel is slightly larger than the state of Vermont, about the size of Belgium. The phrase "from Dan to Beersheba" referred to the northern and southern limits of the kingdom at the height of its glory. It measures about 150 miles from top to bottom. From the coast to the Sea of Galilee is a mere 28 miles; from Gaza to the Dead Sea, 54 miles.

The land was divided into three parts. The northern third was called *Galilee*; the middle, *Samaria*; the lower or southern section, *Judah*. The land lies in the *Fertile Crescent*, whose two tips were Ur of the Chaldees and Egypt. The designation *Palestine* came from the name of Israel's ancient enemy, the Philistines, who once controlled much of the coast. The Romans referred to the territory as *Syro-Palestina*. Only Zechariah called it the *Holy Land* (2:12).

This land (or land-bridge) has always had great military and commercial importance. Here, Egypt once exercised considerable influence, as did Assyria and Babylon.

Israel's brief Golden Age spanned the reigns of kings David and Solomon (1010-930 BC). It ended all too soon with the schism (930 BC), which resulted in a divided kingdom, with Shechem as the northern capital, and Jerusalem the southern. Israel (as the north was called for a time) entered into many alliances with pagan neighbors. The worship of Baal sponsored by the pagan Queen Jezebel added fuel to the fire.

For a time Israel enjoyed prosperity and independence, but its final capital city, Samaria, inevitably doomed, fell in 721 BC. The day of reckoning for Judah, the southern kingdom, came in 587 BC. The ensuing Babylonian Exile ended in 538 BC, thanks to the Persian King Cyrus.

What Is a Prophet?

Throughout history, happenings that interrupted the usual, or deviations from the ordinary, were widely thought to hold a special meaning. To discover that meaning, ancient peoples consulted persons who were credited with special powers of interpretation. They sought guidance in a wide variety of ways: casting lots, shooting arrows and throwing spears, then reading the results. The entrails of sacrificial animals, especially the liver, were given special attention. The flight patterns of birds, or their calls, abnormal births, sudden noises, earthquakes and such phenomena were all believed to convey a meaning which augurs, seers, soothsayers and diviners were able to translate and pass on.

The letter to the Hebrews begins: "In *many* and *various* ways God spoke of old to our fathers by way of the prophets" (1:1). True enough, in Old Testament times God did indeed make his will known in various mysterious ways by *dreams, visions* and *through the prophets*.

In Hebrew a prophet is called a *nabi'*. Our English word *prophet* derives from a Greek word, *prophētēs*. For us, a prophet is commonly thought to be one who predicts the future. In fact, the prophets did this, speaking of such coming events as the *exile*, the *return* from exile, the *Day of the Lord* and *judgment*. Usually, however, prophets dealt with the present.

Prophētēs more properly means *one who speaks for* or *represents someone.* The prophets delivered the Lord's message, speaking in his name. Raising voices of protest against the rejection of traditional values, they championed the ancient faith of their fathers. They did not preach novelty but reform. They were not robots. Grace did not change the sound of their voice nor their way of putting things. It operated through real people, taken just as they were, "warts and all."

The Evolution of Prophecy

Accompanied and assisted by Aaron, Miriam, and others, Moses led his people out of the land of bondage. Then came Gideon, Deborah, Samuel, Elijah, Elisha, and Nathan. All of them might be designated as *early* or *non-writing* prophets. Only Moses, with his higher education, put things down in writing.

With the passage of time, the Chosen People abandoned the nomadic life of the patriarchs and adopted an agricultural way of living. Large cities came into being, and likewise a political awareness of other nations and peoples. In 1050, despite Samuel's opposition to the idea, Israel became a monarchy. In the next century, an enterprising Solomon built royal palaces, promoted commerce, toll-roads and metal working, and through marriage, entered into alliances with foreign powers. Continued contact with pagans and their religious practices proved to be dangerous, and the prophets reacted against tendencies to imitate their neighbors.

During Samuel's time and before Saul became Israel's first king, various "bands" of prophets had appeared on the scene. It is difficult to say much about them, other than the fact that they were religious groups attached to a cultic religion.

Elijah's time (850 BC) saw the appearance of the *sons of the prophets*. The name suggests a blood-relationship, but they were more probably pious groups of men, with some sort of religious connection with Carmel, Bethel, or Gilgal. Clashing at times with the prophets of Baal, they nursed the flame of religious reform.

The Bible often refers to the *high-places*, usually in disparaging terms. These were certain *hilltops* which, because of some peculiarity of terrain (such as an odd rock-formation or an unusual tree, for example), were popularly thought to be places where contact might be made with gods who had visited that very spot.

Pagan rites centering upon life, death, and rebirth were carried out on and around the high-places. The sound of flutes, cymbals, drums and tambourines tended to induce a religious frenzy that sometimes caused participants to whirl about like dervishes. They would thus become god-filled *(enthusiasts)* or *ecstatic* (entranced) instruments of the divine will. Not surprisingly, there were professional prophets among this number. Once, while searching for his father's missing donkeys, the future King Saul happened upon such a group and was caught up in a "prophetic state."

Around 750 BC a new type of prophet appeared, differing from the others in that he had been *called*. He was a *prophet by vocation*. Isaiah 6, Jeremiah 1, and Ezekiel 1 are fascinating autobiographical accounts of personal encounters with God.

What actually transpired on those occasions when a mere mortal was commissioned to speak for the Lord? Modern mystics like Catherine of Siena and Teresa of Avila confess the inability of human speech to do justice to the experience of an awareness of God's presence. It was something extraordinary to be sure, inexpressible, irresistible, and incredibly energizing. From that moment on, those "called" by God become living dynamos concerned only with doing his will.

The prophets were drawn from many different levels of society. A dedicated Samuel served the Lord at the sanctuary in Shiloh. Hosea lived in the Bethel area. Amos tended sheep south of Bethlehem. Isaiah, an aristocrat and a statesman, was a big-city man. Micah was a farmer, Jeremiah a celibate Jerusalem priest, and Ezekiel a widower. Habakkuk was a thinker, Haggai a man in public office. Nahum was a very angry man, while pedigreed Zephaniah was somber and austere. All had different personalities.

Unlike their pagan counterparts, who made a living by sensing what was politically and practically expedient, the true prophets spoke only when a divine influxus was upon them. This varied timewise from prophet to prophet. In contrast to Isaiah and Jeremiah, Amos seems to have had a brief career. There were also periods when no prophetic voice was to be heard at all.

It was not clear how prophets came to be recognized as such. Elijah wore a "garment of haircloth" (2 Kings 1:8), and Isaiah (20:2) wore "sackcloth" around his waist, and sandals. Zechariah (13:4) spoke of a "hairy mantle." But the items here mentioned were common wear for shepherds and ascetics, and it is unlikely that the prophets gained recognition by their clothing. It was when what they foretold actually happened, that people began to take them seriously.

The fact that some prophetic predictions were not fulfilled at all may be variously explained. If a prophecy had been couched in conditional terms, that fact has to be taken into consideration. Thus, "Do this, or else..." does not call for a threatened punishment *if* the conditions were fulfilled. When for example the city of Niniveh and its king (and all its animals!) did penance at the preaching of Jonah, that city (much to the prophet's annoyance) was spared destruction.

On the other hand, some favorable predictions (Hos 14:5-9) were also not fulfilled. Samaria was never to be restored to its former glory, nor Jerusalem to its former splendor. Why? Human speech does not always convey God's utterance clearly. His words always say at the very least that good will triumph over evil, but the "how" of that victory remains shrouded in mystery.

One tends to think that prophets saw the future in clear detail. Isaiah announced that "the virgin" would conceive and bear a child (7:14). This prophecy would not be fulfilled for another 750 years, when Mary gave birth to her son Jesus.

God alone knew what Isaiah's words really meant, and what they would one day be understood to have meant. God's messengers did not need to understand everything the message entailed.

Prophetic Trials

The prophetic office was not passed on from father to son, but was exercised following a sudden grace. The prophets demanded attention because they spoke in God's name. Such a claim naturally aroused wonder and skepticism. The prophets dared criticize the-way-things-were, inviting their hearers to "Hear the word of the Lord!" What they said actually flowed from traditions that traced back to Moses. In calling for a return to the ancient faith and its moral code, the prophets identified themselves as reformers, rather than innovators.

It took a great deal of courage to criticize kings for

their policies, and contemporaries for their way of life. Inevitably the prophets' criticism aroused deep and violent resentment. The prophets were unmoved by this, and continued their course.

The prophet Elijah announced to King Ahab of Israel, a worshipper of Baal, that the Lord was going to send a drought upon the land. So it happened. Somewhat later Ahab caught sight of the prophet and gave vent to his royal displeasure. "Is it you, you *troubler of Israel?*" (1 Kings 18:17), he growled. It was the kind of question that could make one's blood run cold.

After the battle of Megiddo (609), Jeremiah's remarks about royal policy got him thrown into a dark, slimy cistern and left there overnight, undoubtedly a frightful experience. Fortunately, Jeremiah's friends were able to haul him out alive the next morning (Jer 38).

The prophets were not mere seers or diviners (divination was strictly prohibited in Israel). They sought to raise the minds of their hearers to a spiritual plane and to make room in life for a God who wished to be adored, worshipped, and obeyed. They tirelessly proclaimed God's supremacy. That was basic to the ancient faith of Israel.

One studies the prophets to learn what they had to say, and to be inspired by their heroic deeds. They helped prepare the world for the Messiah to come.

The Prophets in Action

Totally convinced of their identity as God's spokesmen, the prophets often invited their countrymen to listen, saying: "Thus says the Lord," or "Hear the word of the Lord." They spoke with conviction and saw to it that God's *oracles* got a hearing. Their versatility and skill deserve our admiration. They made their share of *threats*, but they also knew how to give *comfort*. At times they wore their feelings on their sleeve, employing a special literary form called the *lament* to express their unhappiness. Traditional enemies were sometimes the targets of savage *taunt-songs* and fierce *dirges*. Malachi contains lively arguments presented as dialogues with an adversary.

Isaiah, Jeremiah, and Ezekiel made extensive use of mime, performing strange, symbolic acts: publicly smashing a clay pot, or shaving one's hair and beard in order to attract attention.

These intriguing personalities differed greatly, yet shared several important aspects.

2. Prophetic Styles

Four major concerns surface in prophetic literature. They appear, then disappear only to crop up again. Different one from the other, they are so interrelated that one can hardly speak of any one of them without touching upon the others. The themes are: *Prophecy, the Messiah, Eschatology, and the Apocalyptic.*

A Look at Prophecy

The prophetic writings came into being slowly, in response to various crises. It was a type of literature that was difficult to cope with, yet somehow very important despite its obscurity.

Prophecy is quite often associated with a mysterious foreknowledge of the future. Actually the primary function of the prophets was to restrain kings (from idolatry) and to admonish their own countrymen, who were lamentably well-versed in the usual sins of prosperity: dishonesty, fraud, and cruelty toward the poor and defenseless (widows and children). They addressed a situation in which religion often served as a cloak for sin.

On occasion the prophets' words appeared to suggest something that transcended the present moment, as when they spoke about a mysterious future figure, *a Messiah* who was to come. He would set up a glorious *kingdom* where justice would reign and Zion would again know glory. A kingdom of *peace and prosperity* would be established on the *Day of the Lord*. In God's own time a *King* born of the line of David but surpassing Moses and Solomon and Elijah in wisdom and strength, would enter his royal city seated on the back of a humble donkey. Isaiah spoke of *the* virgin whose son would be called *Emmanuel*. Second-Isaiah wrote of a remarkable *Servant of the Lord* who would die for others' sins. However nebulous all this was, it was at the same time credible, and though deferred, kept hope alive across the centuries.

The Messiah and Messianism

The Hebrew word *Messiah* (in Greek, *Christ*), means *anointed*. From ancient times it was the custom to *anoint* priests and kings with oil. A solemn public anointing indicated that the person so treated was a special person endowed with authority and deserving of respect. Traces of this ancient symbolism linger today.

The word *Messiah* did not always have the religious connotation it has today. The Jews of old looked upon their anointed king as God's earthly viceroy, committed to carrying out the divine will. Yet the kings and the kingdom would disappear. When that happened, long meditation on the sacred writings led to the accumulation of promises concerning *One Who Was to Come*, that is, *the Messiah*, and his glorious kingdom.

The Messiah would be *from the line of David*. Not only would he be a *king*, he would also be God's *son*. He would be a *priest* after the order of Melchisedek that is, *eternal* (the Bible mentions neither the birth nor the death of Melchisedek), and *glorious*. Such titles were deeply significant.

The prospect of a future king of Judah to whom all nations and peoples of the world would be subject, and who would make up for all the hardships endured by his people, was enormously attractive and consoling. Expectations of an *earthly king*, coupled with thoughts of the *Day of the Lord*, rose to fever pitch during the period of Roman domination. Jesus was once asked if he was the one "who had come [to free us]?" On the basis of such expectation, two revolts against Rome would be mounted (one in 66-70 and the other in 132-135 AD), both of them unsuccessful.

Living long after these events, we see that prophecies were sometimes fulfilled in ways far different from what had been expected. The glorious king to come would indeed be triumphant, but through suffering and death! Second Isaiah spoke of the *Servant of the Lord*, accepting an expiatory role as God's way of insuring a sacrifice that would satisfy for the sins of all mankind. The kingdom of the Messiah thus had a moral aspect.

David, anointed by Samuel (1 Sam 16:13), had played an important part in Israel's history. To this talented, successful, and beloved ruler, extravagant promises had been made: Nathan the prophet had clearly stated that a father-son relationship existed between David and the Lord (2 Sam 7:14). David and his kingdom were to endure forever (Ps 2:7; 110:4)!

In reality, these promises of glory could not be fulfilled in an ordinary way, for David's line ended when the last king, Zedekiah, was marched off into exile.

Religious thinkers pondered over the fact that the return from captivity in 538 BC brought with it neither king nor glory. Yet Nathan's words (and the promises made to the first man in Genesis 3:15) could not be dismissed lightly. After much reflection, the thinkers concluded that the Messiah would indeed come to establish a kingdom, but its chief characteristics would be justice and peace. This remarkable event was to occur on the Day of the Lord, at the end of time.

Eschatology

Eschaton means *end*, and the word *eschatology* refers to a consideration of the *last* things, that is, of things that are to take place at the end of time. Beginning with Amos, the prophets were intensely interested in *the Day* when the Lord would appear, manifesting himself in power, might, and glory. The *Last Day* would be a day of vindication and judgment for all the world.

Feverish calculations based on Bible texts and apocalyptic literature have led to a proliferation of ancient and modern sects whose leaders periodically (and unsuccessfully) announce the date when the world will end and glory be made manifest.

The Apocalyptic

Revelation, the last book of the New Testament, was for generations called the *Apocalypse. Apocalyptic,* an adjectival form, refers to a type of literature that was extremely popular from 200 BC to about 100 AD. Even today it continues to attract a wide spectrum of enthusiastic readers.

People who live in an intensely complicated and competitive world are always on the lookout for simple solutions to problems. Apocalyptic literature promises that good will always triumph over evil. Reading it is almost like watching an animated cartoon, wherein there is little dialogue but plenty of action. The issue, however, is never left in doubt. A happy ending is assured. A Messiah does not even enter into the picture. Nor is anything said about the Church and its mission. The battle is between goodness and the forces of evil, with a foregone conclusion.

Many have used the apocalyptic Scriptures in announcing the imminent end of the world and the destruction of the Church. But this is to overlook the fact that the Bible flows from the Church, and not the other way around. Important as the Bible is, it nowhere claims to contain such information.

Apocalyptic literature is simplicity itself. It speaks in multiple visions of the final battle between good and evil. The account of this battle is accredited to certain privileged *seers*, like Moses, Enoch, etc., who *saw* it all happen. It is all over but the shouting.

The apocalyptic abounds in lurid detail. The fearful evil monsters which come out of the sea are thinly veiled references to the great world powers: Assyria, Persia, Greece, and Rome. What was being said in these tales was that Israel's enemies would surely be brought low and destroyed. Signs in the heavens and terrifying upheavals on earth will attend the titanic struggle. With the triumph of good, the sinful world will disappear.

The Bible (Is 24-27, Dan, Zech 9-14, Mt 24, Mk 13, and Lk 21) contains traces of apocalyptic imagery. Some of the best elements in prophetic teaching appear in apocalyptic sections of the other books: God controls everything that happens and will reward those who keep his laws. Good will prevail in the end. God's kingdom *will* prevail.

By introducing the world to its spiritual dimensions, the prophets engendered a faith and hope that would survive political ruin, defeat, and even Exile. Prophetic teachings about the *remnant* (Amos 5:15) and the coming of God's kingdom have stirred up faith, profound hope, and confidence in God's power to save his beloved people. But in the prophets the apocalyptic element is muted and kept under control.

The Land of the Prophets

3. The Individual Prophets

Amos, the Pioneer Prophet

Amos, first in a brilliant line of Hebrew prophets, came from Tekoa, a town in Judah five miles south of Bethlehem. He was just an ordinary shepherd until the day the Lord commanded him: "Go, prophesy to my people Israel."

Amos appeared toward the end of the reign of Jeroboam II, king of Israel (786-746). Other famous people of the time were three Assyrian kings: Tiglath-Pilesar III (745-727), Shalmanezer (726-721), and the greatest of the empire-builders, Sargon II (721-705), who would bring about the fall of Samaria (721). Nebuchadnezzar the Babylonian (604-562) should also be mentioned; Jerusalem fell into his hands in 587 BC.

Part of the background is as follows:

Solomon, an able administrator, had gerrymandered the kingdom of David into twelve districts, each of which was to support the Temple and royal household in Jerusalem for one month of the year. Judah being royal territory, was exempt from this levy.

Shechem, a city halfway between Jerusalem and the Sea of Galilee, lay in the territory of Ephraim, the largest and most influential of the twelve tribes.

After the death of Solomon, his son, Rehoboam, journeyed to Shechem to be proclaimed king. He was deluged with complaints about his father's tax-system. Following the advice of his younger advisers, Rehoboam not only refused to lighten the burden, but promised to increase it. His decision provoked a violent reaction. With repeated shouts of: "To your tents, O Israel!" (1 Kings 12:16), the ten northern tribes seceded. This was schism. The kingdom was divided.

The leader of the rebellion was Jeroboam, an Ephraimite who became king of all Israel. He soon revealed himself to be a religious renegade, setting up two golden calves, one in Dan and one in Bethel, so that his subjects might worship God without going up to Jerusalem. However, the images which originally indicated the presence of the invisible God, soon became themselves objects of worship. The result: idolatry.

The break between the two kingdoms (Israel and Judah) was final. Israel's king built temples on the *high places*, and his subjects prayed there to Baal, a pagan god. To make matters worse, Jeroboam I enjoyed a long and prosperous reign (931-910 BC), and was thus able to consolidate his policies. As time went on, the rift between Israel and Judah grew ever deeper.

It took courage then for Amos, a southerner, to show his face in Bethel, which lay in enemy territory. If a diplomat were to visit another country and there publicly denounce its social injustice and the government authorities responsible for it, he would likewise learn about chilly receptions!

Bethel lies about 25 miles north of Tekoa. Soon after arriving there, Amos voiced his disapproval at what he saw. He was doubtlessly reported at once to Jeroboam II (783-743). It was at Bethel that one of the great encounters of history took place. There, the fierce but articulate sheep-herder called Amos was given a public tongue-lashing by Amaziah, the priest of Baal, for daring to say that Jeroboam the king would one day die by the sword and Israel would be driven into captivity! He was contemptuously ordered off the premises dedicated to Baal, told to go back where he came from, and advised never again to show his face in Bethel.

But Amos had courage and stood his ground, disavowing his connection with a prophetic guild. A shepherd and cultivator of sycamore trees, he had come to Bethel because "the Lord took me...and said to me, 'Go, Prophesy to my people Israel'" (7:15). To the king he sent this message: "Your wife, your children, and you shall fall by the sword, and Israel shall be exiled far from the land" (cf. 7:17).

This is all we know of Amos' public ministry. The encounter may have been brief, but it was highly dramatic. We learn much more about this prophet by reading his magnificent "book."

Amos, the vigorous rustic, possessed a colorful style and expressed himself with unusual power. He used many styles: threats, warnings, reproach, sarcasm. He made good use of rhythm and refrain, and handled parallelism effectively. His imagery grew out of his life. He had more than once heard lions roaring in the night, had experienced drought and heat, and had seen the havoc caused by voracious locusts. In Amos the desert bloomed, producing a poetic genius.

Amos the man is impressive, but his book was not

well put together. First, the nations are told a few things (1-2). More warnings and threats (3-5) follow, but the flow (7-9) is interrupted by the "encounter" we have mentioned (7:10-17). Over all, his dominant theme is one of doom and destruction, but the book ends with a striking description of the messianic kingdom (9:11-15). The contrast in tone is so startling that some scholars consider these verses a later addition.

Amos opens with a numerical device (For three crimes...and for four...) designed to capture attention. Warnings of punishment are aimed in turn at Aram, Tyre, Philistia, Edom, Ammon, Moab, Judah, and Israel. The order in which these nations are called to judgment is ingenious. First, the enemy countries encircling the land, including, unexpectedly, even Judah, and lastly, climactically, sinful Israel! All artfully done.

Amos uses the refrain to good effect. One of these, *Lo 'ashibennu* (= I will not revoke my word) is repeated no less than eight times in the first two chapters. Another is "Yet you did not return to me," appearing five times in chapter 4.

Shepherds sometimes ventured into towns or villages to sell their sheep or to purchase supplies. What Amos saw in Bethel disgusted him: injustice everywhere, with dishonest merchants using short weights, the rich heartlessly exploiting the poor and sleeping in ivory-inlaid beds (3:15; 6:4). But what angered him most was the way people went through the motions of being religious.

One can imagine the shock and indignation that greeted these stinging words:

> "I hate, I despise your feasts,
> and I take no delight in your solemn assemblies....
> Take away from me the noise of your songs!" (5:21-23)

At first glance these words appear to be a condemnation of ritual and public ceremony, but such a conclusion would be wrong. Religion is not a private affair between oneself and God, but a community project. Human beings are not angels worshipping God in a bodiless way. Ritual has its place. The whole of a man is involved in divine worship; the body has something to contribute. Feasts and solemnities and solemn rituals are visible signs of a worshipper's commitment to God.

Or, at least, they should be. What Amos was denouncing was a mockery of worship. Wholly immersed in material things, many reduced their religious practice to meaningless motions. Amos spoke out against that attitude.

Religion is like a road flanked by ditches. One ditch might be called "Too Little" and the other "Too Much." A traveler must stay in the middle of the road and all will be well. The comparison is useful. Even in the worship of God there can be too much or too little ceremony. It is not as if the ceremony is everything, or devotion simply inward. True worship calls for a reasonable amount of ritual, and a reasonable amount of deliberate awareness of God and acceptance of his will.

Amos described drought, blighted crops, and the plague as warnings from God to sinners. Let them mend their ways. But such warnings often went unheeded. Amos described the Lord as saying, "You did not return to me," and then follows this up with the grim words: "Prepare to meet your God" (4:11-12).

Notwithstanding the persistent note of judgment and condemnation, Amos too has a tender side. We hear him pleading, "O Lord God forgive.... How can Jacob stand? He is so small" (7:2, 5). And not to be overlooked is the fact that Amos heard the Lord refer to Israel as "my people." God cares for all his wayward children.

Amos was the first prophet to speak of the *remnant*, an idea that later prophets would adopt and develop. Divine punishment will always stop short of total destruction. Something, if only a tiny remnant, will always be spared (5:15). One thinks of Elijah's mournful "I only, am left" (1 Kings 19:10). Even a small remnant can signify a hopeful future.

When shall God be victorious? Amos was also the first to introduce the idea of the *Day of the Lord* (5:18-20), a day of darkness, not light, a day of gloom and judgment. During the later exile the Day would become the focus of hope. After the exile it became more and more an important symbol of judgment, of the end of the world.

One cannot but admire Amos' versatility and eloquence. As punishment for the emptiness of religious thought and practice, he wrote, "Behold the days are coming, says the Lord God, when I will send a famine on the land; not a famine of bread, nor a thirst for water, but of hearing the words of the Lord" (8:11). A famine of bread is bad enough, but man does not live on bread alone (Deut 8:3), as another and greater prophet, Jesus, would remind us (Mt 4:4). The day will come when people will hunger and thirst for the word of God.

One best speaks of messianic matters by making use of hyperbole, as Amos does. "In that day I will raise up the booth of David that is fallen.... Behold, the days are coming, says the Lord, when the plowman shall overtake the reaper, and the treader of grapes, him who sows the seed; the mountains shall drip sweet wine, and all the hills shall flow with it" (9:11-13).

These lines clearly attempt to describe something that has never before been seen or even imagined, but which shall one day come to pass. With a stroke of genius Amos envisaged the messianic age in terms meaningful to a farmer. Imagine if one had only to sow seed to have it spring up at once, ripe and ready for the harvest. Farmers and growers of grapes know very well that it takes months to grow a crop. But how different things will be, and how much more wonderful, Amos suggests, in the kingdom of God, who is prodigal with his mercies!

The seed, of course, is God's grace, the word of God, the gospel. So powerful is it that it produces its life-giving effects at once. Such prodigality is found in the sacraments, which give grace each time we receive them.

Hosea, Tragic Lover

Hosea lived about the same time as Amos and may have heard him speak at Bethel. Some twenty years after Amos spoke out, Jeroboam II died. His successors reigned for six months and one month respectively. Thus, Hosea lived in deeply troubled times. He may have still been alive at the fall of Samaria in 721.

Le style, c'est l'homme. A man's writings reveal him to his readers. Amos was harsh and explosive. Hosea, much more sensitive, has been called the first mystic among the prophets.

Hosea often spoke like a farmer about sowing, harvesting, and threshing. He spoke about wheat, flax, oil, and wool. He knew about mending fences, and how calves and heifers behaved. Because of his repeated references to ovens, some have concluded that he might have been a baker!

Amos was a stern, somber person, and his prophecy not at all what we call devotional reading. Hosea is more to our liking. He was a married man whose wife was, alas, unfaithful. Grieving over this, as was natural, he one day saw in a blinding flash, that what was happening in his life was an image of what was taking place in the life of his people. Israel too was unfaithful, an adulteress worshipping idols, running after false gods, abandoning her one, true God.

The prophet saw something else that almost overwhelmed him. He saw that, just as he was willing to forgive his errant wife, God was willing to show mercy and to pardon his sinful people.

It is not known where Hosea was born, but it is certain he was a northerner. He refers to Israel in various ways, calling it Jacob, or Samaria, or (37 times) Ephraim. The cities he mentions, Bethel (equated with Beth-aven, or "House of iniquity"), Gilgal, Gibeah, and Ramah, are all in Israel. He ignores Jerusalem..

We know nothing about Hosea's early life. The Lord had told him to "take a harlot wife" and have children by her. The story is once told in the third person and once in the first. Gomer, the wife, bore him two sons and a daughter.

St. Jerome regarded Gomer as an allegorical figure, but others (Irenaeus, Augustine, and Thomas) felt that Hosea married a real woman. It is most unlikely that she was a common prostitute when Hosea married her, for God cannot command anyone to sin. It is more likely that once married, Gomer acted like a whore. Their three children were given symbolic names: *Jezreel* (= God disperses), *Lo-ruhama* (= Not pitied), and *Lo-'ammi* (= Not my people). For Hosea, all three names aptly apply to Israel.

Hosea's life was a symbol of the husband-wife relationship that existed between God and Israel. God had taken Israel as his spouse. She had not been true to him, but God is a persistent lover. After correcting his beloved he would lead her into the desert, back to those idyllic days when he was Israel's God and Israel was his people.

The political background of Hosea's work influenced its content. Throughout history, the northern kingdom was seldom at peace. While petty kings squabbled among themselves, Assyria grew steadily in power. Menahem of Israel held on to his throne by paying a heavy tribute, 1,000 talents of silver (2 Kings 15) to Pul (the biblical name for Tiglath-Pilesar). He thus acquired a powerful ally, but alas, the Israelite king soon died. At once, plans to form an alliance against Assyria were feverishly discussed.

What of Hosea? Surrounded by fanatic schemers, he turned to God. Readers of his book soon realize where he stood. Idolatry was nothing but adultery, and idolaters deserved to be stripped bare and exposed as shameless harlots.

Where there is no true religion, fallen nature tends to assert itself. For lack of true knowledge of God, ancient peoples had tended to worship nature and its powers. Fertility cults, complete with temple or ritual prostitution, flourished on the *high places* (4:13ff.).

In these bad times, Hosea observed, with a heavy heart: "There is no faithfulness or kindness, and no knowledge of God in the land." Much of the blame for this he attributed to the priests. "My people are destroyed for lack of knowledge" (4:1, 6).

What was this knowledge? Certainly more than information about God. For Hosea, knowledge and love went hand in hand. God was not an intellectual concept, but a *person* who made himself known and shared his love with those linked to him by a covenant. In God one can perceive what Hosea called *hesed*, or a special kind of love that bespoke intimacy, affection and understanding. Terms like *hesed* and *da'ath* (knowledge) are as one; man "knows" God when he observes God's covenant, evinces

gratitude for God's gifts, and returns love for love. Bene-
volence and gratitude should meet. That is how Hosea
saw it.

Israel's sin, for Hosea, was a sin against love. In
11:3-4, he describes in touching terms the tenderness of
God's love for his children, reaching sheer eloquence in
verse 8.

"I led them with cords of compassion,
with the bands of love,
and I became to them as one who eases the yoke...
and I bent down to them and fed them....
How can I give you up, O Ephraim!
How can I hand you over, O Israel!
My heart recoils within me,
my compassion grows warm and tender."

Hosea perceived that love outraged is still love, and
that God is love. Sin then shall not have the last word.
There is a time for a repentance which will be followed
by forgiveness, by a renewal of the covenant.

Hosea's language is strangely compelling. Describ-
ing his people's religious sense, he declared: "Your love
is like a morning cloud, like the dew that goes early
away" (6:4). The land of Israel knows only two seasons,
one rainy and the other dry. During the dry season dawn
often breaks dark, ominous, and threatening rain. Yet the
rain never comes, and the rain-promising clouds gradu-
ally disappear.

Like a true Semite, Hosea shows his skill in parallelism in chapter 9. This characteristically Semitic technique
consists in saying the same thing twice, using parallels.
For example (7:1): "The corruption of Ephraim is revealed, and the wicked deeds of Samaria." Here are four
nouns, each having an "echo." Again in 5:1 "Hear this, O

priests! Give heed, O house of Israel!" As in the wisdom books, parallelism is the rule.

Many phrases from Hosea cling to the memory, as for example: "They sow the wind, and they shall reap the whirlwind" (8:7). Elsewhere, we find such good advice as (14:3) "Take with you words and return to the Lord." Or (10:12) "Sow for yourselves righteousness, reap the fruit of steadfast love."

What more plaintive and revealing line than that of chapter 6 (v. 6): "I desire steadfast love and not sacrifice, the knowledge of God, rather than burnt offerings."

The Book of Hosea had a profound influence on both the Old and the New Testaments. Later prophets were to echo Hosea's teaching that religion must issue from the heart, with the love of God as its driving force.

The New Testament quotes Hosea, and the Liturgy uses his text six times in all. The wedding imagery of God's love for his people will reappear in the major prophets, and Christians here catch a glimpse of the union between Christ and his Church. The idea of a loving union or mystical espousal between Christ and the individual soul is found in the writings of the mystics.

THE DIVIDED KINGDOM

KINGS OF JUDAH	KINGS OF ISRAEL	PROPHETS
Rehoboam 931-913	Jeroboam I 931-910	
Abijah 913-911		
Asa 911-870	Nadab 910-909	
	Baasha 909-886	
	Elah 886-885	
	Zimri 885	
	Omri 885-874	
	Ahab 874-853	
Jehoshaphat 870-848		
Jehoram 848-841	Ahaziah 853-852	
Ahaziah 841	Jehoram 852-841	
Athaliah 841-835	Jehu 841-814	
Joash 835-796	Jehoahaz 814-798	
	Joash 798-783	
Amaziah 796-781		Amos
Uzziah 781-740	Jeroboam II 783-743	Hosea
	Zechariah 743	Isaiah
	Shallum 743	Micah
	Menahem 743-738	
Jotham 740-736	Pekahiah 738-737	
	Pekah 737-732	
Ahaz 736-716	Hoshea 782-724	
	FALL OF SAMARIA 721	

Hezekiah 716-687   FALL OF NINEVEH 612
Manasseh 687-642
Amon 642-640
Josiah 640-609
Jehoahaz 609
Jehoiakim 609-598
Jehoiakin 598
Zedekiah 598-587   FALL OF BABYLON 538
FALL OF JERUSALEM 587
Deportation 587   Zephaniah
THE EXILE 587-538   Jeremiah

Nahum
Habakkuk
Ezekiel

Haggai
Zechariah
Malachi
Joel
Obadiah
Jonah
Daniel

THE PERSIAN PERIOD	538-333 BC
THE HELLENISTIC PERIOD	333-63 BC
THE ROMAN PERIOD	BC 63 -135 AD

Isaiah, the Great Prophet

The prophets were all God-centered men. In contrast to monarchs who loved to glorify themselves on public monuments, the prophets put God first. No prophet did this more eloquently than Isaiah, who is unmatched in breadth of vision. Few pieces of prose in any language can compare with his dramatic description of his call (6:1-13).

One day while praying in the Temple, depressed perhaps by the recent death of King Uzziah (742 BC), Isaiah had a vision. He "saw" the Ancient of Days seated on a royal throne, surrounded by mysterious figures (the seraphim) who were chanting "Holy, Holy, Holy is the Lord of hosts." (The three-fold repetition signifies God's *transcendent holiness*). Next he heard the Lord musing aloud, asking, "Whom shall I send, and who will go for us?" At once, without knowing what he might be getting into, Isaiah responded, "Here I am! Send me."

What a magnificent scene! There was no reluctance on Isaiah's part, no holding back as was the case with Moses and Jeremiah, who dragged their feet at the prospect of becoming prophets. Isaiah was prepared for anything. "Send me!" He was told then to speak to God's people as the accredited mouthpiece of the Lord most high. The Lord had picked the right man, of course. Isaiah was to have a distinguished career. To begin with, he was an aristocrat, comfortable in the presence of important people. Quite obviously he was a man of culture, charm and ability. He had *class*, and would serve for forty years under four kings.

Despite these words of praise, we have to remember that, because Isaiah appeared when he did, his knowledge of God was somewhat limited. The New Testament with its full revelation of God and his plan was yet to appear. This is not said to "put down" the prophet. Quite the contrary. He was a great visionary and prepared the way for the Good News.

The Political Situation

The century in which Isaiah lived was anything but calm. Israel and Judah were both in a precarious position as Egypt and Assyria jockeyed for power and glory.

Assyria was poised on the threshold of its Golden Age. Because of Menahem's payment of tribute, the Assyrian ruler, Tiglath-Pilesar III, had become Israel's ally. A few years after Menahem's death, Pekah of Israel joined with Syria in an anti-Assyrian alliance favored by Egypt. When Jotham of Judah refused to join the coalition, a tense situation developed. Damascus seized Elath, Judah's Red Sea port, and the Philistines retook cities along the coastal plain. Next, a pro-Assyrian party at the Jerusalem court put pressure on the new king, Ahaz, urging him to maintain ties with Assyria. At this precise moment Isaiah intervened, assuring Ahaz not to do this, for it was neither necessary nor beneficial. The alliance of Egypt, Israel and Syria would collapse.

Already a king at only twenty years of age, Ahaz was not inclined to heed a prophet who could only promise him a mysterious "sign." In the end he went to Damascus bearing gifts of gold taken from the Temple in Jerusalem. Ahaz obviously put his trust in the persuasive power of gold. Assyria agreed to protect Judah against the alliance. Returning from his successful mission, Ahaz brought with him a pagan altar which he proceeded to set it up in the Temple of the Lord, for use in pagan worship. Isaiah must have been horrified.

The Virgin and Emmanuel

Unlike Amos, Isaiah spent his whole life in and around the royal city, Jerusalem. His interest was in Zion (another name for Jerusalem, the royal city). One of his most famous prophecies was the "sign" for the house of David that Ahaz spurned: "The virgin shall be with child and bear a son, and she shall name him Emmanuel" (cf. 7:14).

For a closer look at this text, see chapter 4.

Isaian Highlights

The prophecy of Isaiah is truly impressive. On page after page, phrases or sections startle us with their beauty and depth. Here is a list of some memorable passages:

References to the *remnant,* beginning with 1:9.

A plea for *penance.* If one would "cease to do evil, and learn to do good" he would discover: "Though your sins are like scarlet, they shall be as white as snow; though they are red like crimson, they shall become like wool" (1:16-18).

A vision of peace, of what can be: "They shall beat their swords into plowshares, and their spears into pruning hooks" (2:4).

Concerning the idle rich (3:16-26).

The song of the vineyard (5:1-7—compare John 15).

The call of Isaiah (6:1-8).

Shear-jashub = A remnant will remain. The name of Isaiah's second son was *Maher-shalal-hash-baz = Speeds the spoils, hastens the prey.*

The names of the "wonder child" of 9:6 ascribe to him outstanding qualities: wisdom (Solomon), valor (David), authority, fatherly concern for his people, and peace. The Christian liturgy has mined this passage for its riches.

The role of Emmanuel. Of David's line, he shall be a *shoot from the stump of Jesse* (David's father), will have wondrous spiritual gifts, and shall inaugurate a period of idyllic peace (11:1-9).

Chapters 24-27 are an "apocalypse" concerning Zion.

Micah, Man of the Land

The Hebrew prophets ought not to be naively lumped together, as if they were all alike. Actually they are like the stars in the heavens, having much in common, but each different from the others.

Micah may possibly have heard his contemporary, Isaiah, speak. Isaiah was rich and exciting, a sparkling personality; Micah can be pictured as an irate farmer, surprisingly articulate and aware of what was going on. He was the last of the four 8th-century prophets. During his time, three kings ruled over Judah: Jotham, Ahaz, and Hezekiah. This last-named monarch launched a religious reform along the lines Micah had recommended.

Born of ordinary middle-class stock, this prophet was from Moresheth, southwest of Jerusalem. To the east lay Amos' home town, Tekoa, on the edge of the desert and boasting a view of the Dead Sea. To the west were rich, fertile plains that sloped down toward the sea, and the coastal plain.

Today, with our easy access to world news through TV and radio, we may wonder what impact the words and writings of the prophets had on their contemporaries. Some people listen better than they read, and a living speaker generally makes a more vivid impression. In reacting to the evils of their times, the prophets by word of mouth or in their writings revived the still, small voice of conscience in their listeners.

Micah was one of those powerful speakers. A hundred years later, Jeremiah (26:18) would save his own life by quoting Micah 3:12 concerning the dreadful fate awaiting Zion.

The stirrings of Assyrian expansionism caused much uneasiness everywhere. Jotham of Judah had rejected invitations to join the anti-Assyrian Syro-Ephraimitic coalition, and Ahaz, his successor, had aligned himself with Assyria.

Micah was apparently not very politically minded. He said that God would punish Samaria and Judah, and with considerable force he denounced the excesses of the rich, who stopped at nothing in order to increase their holdings.

Religious consciousness in Micah's time was clearly at a low ebb, as were public and private morality. The "high places" with their attendant pagan deities and immoral practices were flourishing.

Micah had courage. He denounced both the leaders of the people and the venality of false prophets. Jerusalem (= Zion), he predicted, would be reduced to rubble. Yet there was still hope. Peace would come, and swords and spears would be transformed into instruments of peace. More than that, out of *Bethlehem* there was to come *a Messiah* to lead his people. In these two texts, (4:1-5 and 5:1-2), Micah expresses himself in terms much like those used by Isaiah.

Micah manifests another and constructive side. He often refers to a *remnant* that will be saved (2:12; 4:6; 5:7, 7:18). Using only a remnant, the merciful God who does not even need a remnant, can and will restore all things. What God desires is a religion of the spirit: worshippers must "do justice" (Amos had said that), "love kindness" (as Hosea had taught), and "walk humbly with your

God" (6:8), as Isaiah said. Here was and is a thumbnail summation of the prophetical teaching on religion.

And then there is also a splendid promise of forgiveness and restoration (7:19):

"He will again have compassion upon us,
he will tread our iniquities under foot.
Thou wilt cast all our sins
into the depths of the sea."

Micah singles out Bethlehem-Ephrathah for praise (5:1-4), for from it came the ancient Davidic dynasty. He says:

"From you shall come forth for me
one who is to be ruler in Israel,
whose origin is from of old, from ancient days...
when she who is in travail has brought forth...."

Of him who was to be born there of the mother of the Messiah, Micah notes, "He shall be our peace" (cf. 5:4).

Zephaniah and the *Dies Irae*

Zephaniah has the longest pedigree mentioned by any of the prophets. He seems to have had royal blood in his veins, being descended from Hezekiah (1:1). Full of zeal for the Lord of hosts, Zephaniah directed his fierce shafts against foreign cults. Due to Assyrian influences, star-worship and idolatry had spread throughout Israel during the reigns of Manasseh and Amon (687-640).

This prophecy was written before the fall of Nineveh (612). As the power of Assyria declined, lesser nations felt encouraged to undertake projects hitherto unthinkable. Thus Josiah launched a religious reform around 621 BC. Zephaniah, however, seems not to have known about the reform, so it is probable that he wrote before that date.

The later prophets read and pondered over the works of their predecessors. The Book of Zephaniah has all the earmarks of a compilation. Its theme, the *Day of the Lord* and *the remnant*, goes back to Amos. Zephaniah too pictured that day as dark and somber, a *dies irae* (1:14f.), a day of wrath. The prophet spoke of the Lord as exploring Jerusalem with lamps (1:12); no evil-doer would escape his punishment.

The prophets expressed their views in a somewhat violent but typically Semitic fashion, that is, with such force and energy that any other view seemed relatively unimportant. Vehement expressions tell us a great deal about individual emphases and preferences.

Amos had harshly announced the coming judgment, but he had also introduced the idea of a remnant that might survive (5:15). Hosea was the prophet of divine love and mercy. Isaiah stressed God's holiness and a judgment which the remnant would survive. Micah mentioned holiness and humility. There is definitely a somberness about Zephaniah.

Seemingly fascinated by the idea of a fiery judgment, Zephaniah reveals in his short prophecy (53 verses) , his familiarity with Amos and the remnant, as well as with Micah's words about the meek the humble. He also owes much to Isaiah, who had combined the notions of judgment (34:8) with that of a remnant (10:20-22; 37:32).

Like John the Baptist, Zephaniah was an intense, austere man. The reader will find nothing in his pages about peace, hope, love of God, or forgiveness. Only in the eight concluding verses of his prophecy is mention made of peace and joy, and only there does he suggest that bad days can be in fact a period of purification:

"I will leave in the midst of you
a people humble and lowly.
They shall seek refuge in the name of the Lord" (3:12).

"I will bring you home....
When I restore your fortunes before your eyes" (3:20).

Jeremiah and Personal Sufferings

Jeremiah came upon the scene a hundred years after the first group of prophets—Amos, Hosea, Isaiah, and Micah. Born and raised in Anathoth (about four miles north and east of Jerusalem), he may have been about thirty years old when the Lord called him. The year was 626 BC.

King Josiah (640-609), following the discovery in 621 of the book of the Law (Deuteronomy) during a renovation of the Temple, launched a sweeping religious reform. Pagan intrusions were ruthlessly set aside, the covenant with the Lord was renewed, and the Passover was again celebrated according to the ancient rules.

The years 625-612 mark the decline and fall of Assyria. Josiah capitalized on this by seizing Samaria, Bethel, and other cities to restore the ancient kingdom of David. However, Josiah died while fighting at Megiddo. Sirach sang his praises (49:1-4).

Jeremiah's inaugural vision was a dramatic, unforgettable experience. In it he learned that, before he had even been born, the Lord had prepared, shaped, and dedicated him to be his prophet. Like Moses, Gideon, and others (but unlike the great Isaiah), Jeremiah was unenthused at the prospect and tried to get out of it. He pleaded his youth and his inability to speak well, but to no avail. He would have to do the Lord's bidding. He would have to do the Lord's work throughout the most agitated period of the nation's history. And he did.

Tender and sensitive by nature, Jeremiah was told not to marry. His orders were to "pluck up and to break down, to destroy and to overthrow, to build and to plant" (1:10). As an announcer of calamity, he was judged to be a coward and a defeatist. He was roughly treated, but he persisted, and in the end turned out to be, as the Lord had promised, "an iron pillar, and bronze walls" (1:18).

Jeremiah found his task unappealing. He knew discouragement, and cursed the day he was born! Made fun of and laughed at, he resolved to keep his mouth shut and not speak in the Lord's name. Then, as he relates, the word of God became "in my heart as it were a burning fire...I am weary with holding it in, and I cannot" (20:9). So he began again.

In his "confessions" (11:18-25; 12:1-6; 15:10-21; 17:9-18; 18:19-23; and 20:7-12), we catch glimpses of Jeremiah's wrestling with the Lord, and with himself. He voiced his innermost feelings, his self-doubts, anxieties and bewilderment at the ways of God. In these autobiographical sections of his writings, we learn something of what it was like to be a prophet. Jeremiah complained to the Lord, argued with him, and called upon him for help. It grieved him to see the wicked prosper (12:1) while he, doing the Lord's work, was having such a bad time. The Lord refused to pamper him; even greater trials lay ahead (12:5). But his enemies would not prevail (1:19).

Jeremiah was typical of his times. He heaped curses on his enemies and urged the Lord to gather them as sheep for the slaughter, and to visit upon them famine, plague, the sword, and death. More than anything he wanted to see the Lord's vengeance in action (12:20).

Jeremiah's plight became more tolerable when he was joined by Baruch. This disciple became a staunch ally and assistant (chapters 36 and 45), who like Mark, Timothy and others shine while serving the cause of a greater personality. Without a Baruch, we might never have had the Jeremiah we know and admire.

The Early Period—626-609

The great reform sparked by the discovery of the book of the Law is duly recorded in 2 Kings 22-23. When King Josiah died, however, pagan practices promptly reappeared. Jeremiah was grieved as he saw his people digging for themselves "broken cisterns, that can hold no water" (2:13).

Many miles to the northeast, exciting things were happening. Assyria's collapse, unbelievably swift, and the fall of proud Nineveh, which was literally wiped from the face of the earth, were newsworthy events that galvanized the world.

From 609-605

While fighting the Egyptian pharaoh Neco at Megiddo in 609, good King Josiah was killed. He was succeeded by Jehoahaz, whom Neco replaced with Jehoiakim. Neco was defeated by the Babylonians in 605 at Carchemish. Some twenty years later, the Babylonians (= Chaldeans), led by Nebuchadnezzar, would be knocking at the gates of Jerusalem. Jeremiah would witness it all.

Chapters 4-10; 13-17; 22:10-12; 26; 46 apply to this period. Passages of sheer beauty alternate with ominous sounds—the invasion from the north. It was a fitting time to turn to God.

From 605-598

After the battle of Carchemish, Jeremiah composed an exultant poem (46:1-12). Megiddo was revenged. But he predicted that the people of Judah would be enslaved in Babylon for 70 years (25:1-14). In rude, stirring language, Jeremiah described a bowl of foaming wine, a wine of divine wrath, which all nations would taste (25:1, 30-38).

After Carchemish, Nebuchadnezzar marched as far south as the Nile Delta (Pelusium). He then hurried back to Babylon, leaving Jehoiakim of Judah in Jerusalem as his vassal. He would return.

Jeremiah had once before spoken of the destruction of the Holy City, and was saved from death only when a similar prophecy by Micah was recalled (26). When Jeremiah sent Baruch to read his message (36), the king showed his displeasure, cutting off portions of the scroll as they were read and feeding them to the fire!

Jeremiah recalled how potters sometimes revised their plans to suit the texture of the clay. If Judah would only mend her ways, he declared, God could change his plans about his people. Let Judah repent, and return to the Lord (18).

Another symbolic action (19-20), the deliberate public smashing of a clay pot, as a prophecy of the Lord's forthcoming punishment for Judah, led to Jeremiah's arrest. He was scourged and kept overnight in jail, in the stocks! Released the next morning, he did not recant; instead he spoke of the coming exile. And he poured out his unhappiness in a marvelous passage that reveals his inner turmoil. "You have duped me, Lord" (cf. 20:7-19). It is one of the most moving lines in the prophet's "confessions."

The Fall of Jerusalem

Returning from Babylon, Nebuchadnezzar laid siege to Jerusalem. King Jehoiakim died at the outbreak of hostilities, and was replaced by his eighteen-year-old son Jehoiachin, who ruled for only three months before being deported to Babylon. Along with the king and his mother there marched the king's officials, the nobles, men of valor, craftsmen, smiths, and at least one priest— a man named Ezekiel, destined to be a prophet in exile.

Nebuchadnezzar then placed Zedekiah, the ex-king's uncle, on the throne. The last and most tragic of Judah's kings, his reign was a succession of errors. He granted audiences to anti-Babylonian plotters, but also consulted Jeremiah, now beginning, as the Lord had foretold (cf. 12:5) "to compete with horses."

During the last days of the kingdom of Judah, Jeremiah continued to produce oracles and sayings which ran counter to the fantasies of the anti-Babylonian schemers who had flocked to the court from neighboring countries.

During these tense times, Jeremiah spoke of the good figs, that is, the good people who had been carried off to exile. The Lord would take care of them. But the bad figs (Zedekiah and his followers) were destined for destruction.

Reacting fiercely against false prophets, Jeremiah delivered this message: "Is not my word like fire, says the Lord, like a hammer which breaks the rock in pieces?" (23:29) One dramatic encounter involved wooden yokes, worn to make a point, or broken to pieces (28:1ff.).

Jerusalem fell in July, 587. The king attempted flight but was captured near Jericho. Jeremiah had been right all along. His chains were removed and he was allowed to stay wherever he wished. He moved to Mizpah (five miles northwest of Jerusalem), where his friend Gedeliah had been established as governor by the Babylonians. It was probably at Mizpah that Jeremiah composed two exultant poems (chapters 30-31). The first of these was a joyful promise of restoration. A messianic king of David's line would appear (30:8-9).

The second poem, especially 31:27-30, 35-36, contains the doctrine of *individual responsibility* or *retribution*, and a teaching about *a new covenant* or *alliance* under which all shall know the Lord, for the law will be written, not on stone, but in living hearts.

These verses constitute the longest Old Testament quotation used in the New Testament. They are the crowning-point of Jeremiah's career, and indeed, the high-point of Old Testament teaching. Our term "New Testament" derives from this passage. The graces and blessings of God are now available to all under conditions incomparably superior to those of another and older day. God has not disappointed humankind; he has kept his word.

No single verse of the Bible says everything. It would be a mistake, then, to reject organized religion and the priesthood on the basis of Jeremiah 31. Jesus' words ("Do this...often") at the Last Supper renders such an interpretation untenable.

A messianic text is one that says something about the Messiah and/or his work. Jeremiah 31:22 is an intriguing text, but is it messianic? St. Jerome thought that it referred to Jesus and his mother Mary. Here is the text in a common translation:

"The Lord has created a new thing on the earth:
a woman protects a man."

A new and slightly enhanced translation reads:
"The woman must/shall encompass the man *with devotion*"

(NAB). It is difficult to understand the verse without the addition of these two words. The Lord once surrounded Israel (woman) with mercy and devotion; in the new age, the reverse will be true, God's people will love and serve him.

Jeremiah's last days were troubled and, as usual, unpredictable. At Mizpah, Gedeliah, the governor appointed by the Babylonians, was murdered by discontented patriots. Shortly thereafter a group of Judahites fled to Egypt, taking Jeremiah and Baruch with them. There they would die.

To the last, Jeremiah affirmed Judah's infidelity to the Lord. From a human point of view, he was a complete failure. As time went on, however, he grew in stature as "the" prophet, and came to be considered as possibly the Messiah (Mt 16:14). By the time of 2 Maccabees (2:5), he had become a national saint. Since then, he has been recognized as the most human of the prophets and a source of much consolation.

Nahum and Sweet Revenge

The Book of Nahum was written between 621 and 612 BC. The first date marks the beginning of Josiah's reform; the second, that of the fall of Nineveh, the capital of Assyria. Although quite short, Nahum's prophecy is greatly admired for the vividness of its imagery.

Assyria had grown steadily in power over a period of 300 years, and had come to dominate all of Mesopotamia. Ancient monuments testify both to Assyria's glory and to its systematic policy of cruelty. The frightful atrocities committed by Hitler and the Gestapo, or by the Russian KGB in Stalin's time, were modern counterparts of Assyrian brutality.

Isaiah predicted (10:12) the downfall of the arrogant king of Assyria; Nahum looked forward to that event with passionate impatience. God's people would survive, but nations and peoples without spiritual vision would inevitably perish. And so indeed it came about. Thebes in Upper Egypt (= No-Amon of 3:8), was destroyed by the Assyrians in 665. Nineveh, east of the Tigris and near modern Mosul, fell in 612 BC. Jerusalem would likewise fall, in 586 BC.

Habakkuk, Daring Questioner

The late 7th century before Christ had witnessed a number of world-shaking events. The unthinkable had happened. Mighty Assyria, whose power had reached from India to Egypt, had collapsed. Its proud capital, Nineveh, had fallen (612 BC), Egypt was busy assessing the sudden appearance of Chaldean (Babylonian) might in the area.

In 609 BC, "good" King Josiah of Judah had died in battle at Megiddo. Four years later, in the famous battle of Carchemish—65 miles northeast of Aleppo (Syria)—the Babylonian King Nebuchadnezzar defeated an Egyptian army led by the Pharaoh Neco, and thus become master of all Mesopotamia. In 597 he was to lay siege to Jerusalem, and again in 587 BC, when the city would fall into his hands and a final group of exiles would be taken to Babylon.

From a moral, religious, and political point of view, things could hardly have been worse. Josiah was succeeded by his son Jehoahaz (who ruled 3 months) and then by Jehoiakim, whose reign was characterized by corruption, extravagance, and idolatry. Jeremiah would suffer for his criticism of it (see Jer 38).

It was at this point in time (605-597) that Habakkuk prophesied. According to one tradition he came from Beth-Sakariyeh, a town ten miles southwest of Jerusalem, and was perhaps one of the singers who assisted priests. His strange name may have meant a plant. His words reveal him as a man of tender heart (2:16f.), but he did something no one had ever dared do before: he asked God to explain himself! Did God *have* to use the Babylonians to punish the people for their sins? They were as bad as, or worse than, the Assyrians!

The surprising thing about this is that God replied! He explained that he was using the Chaldeans as a chastening rod, an instrument of divine justice. Bad as things appeared, the just man had no cause to fear. He had only to hold fast and not lose heart, and he would live.

St. Thomas Aquinas discussed in his impressive *Summa* the only two objections he could think of against the existence of God. One of these was the existence of evil. Habakkuk was the first ancient to raise the "question of evil." *Why* is Habakkuk's word. He felt that religion should ask realistic questions, and questioning like his own led to the production of one of Israel's noblest bits of literature, the Book of Job (cf. Job 33+).

As the Jews had no concept of a world beyond time, present recompense was their chief preoccupation. But the sufferings of the innocent pose a problem for us as they did for Habakkuk (1:1-4). The cure (Chaldea) had turned out to be worse than the disease (Assyria). Why so? (1:12-17), the prophet asked.

We learn something here about the prophetic technique. Habakkuk climbed up on his watchtower (2:1-4), and waited for the Lord's next move. He was to learn that character alone abides; the evils of tyrants disappear, but *the righteous shall live by his faith.* In the long run, this is true. History proves it.

Chapter 3 is a magnificent religious lyric filled with poetic reminiscences of Hebrew history. Verses 17-18 are a beautiful expression of the prophet's faith, and one the reader will undoubtedly appreciate and approve.

"Though the fig tree do not blossom
nor fruit be on the vines,
the produce of the olive fail
and the fields yield no food,
the flock be cut off from the fold
and there be no herd in the stalls,
yet I will rejoice in the Lord,
I will joy in the God of my salvation.
God, the Lord, is my strength;
he makes my feet like hinds' feet,
he makes me tread upon my high places."

Ezekiel, the Strange One

Ezekiel was a priest-in-exile. He lived near Babylon, one of the show-places of the ancient world. There a *ziggurat*, or tower with nine sets of steps, rose to the heavens. There too stood a grandiose temple in honor of Bel (or Marduk, the chief god of the city). The royal palace became famous for its *hanging gardens*. Nebuchadnezzar had built double walls around this city, and irrigation projects using water from the nearby Euphrates contributed to the city's beauty and prosperity.

One day while standing near the great canal Chebar, Ezekiel had a strange vision. As he put it: "The word of the Lord came to me...and the hand of the Lord came upon me" (cf. 1:3). It must have startled the prophet to learn that Israel's God would manifest himself on foreign soil!

Ezekiel's inaugural vision was so strange and difficult to understand that for a time it was almost off-limits; it was not to be read by anybody under thirty years of age. It is difficult to describe an experience of God. Ezekiel made the attempt, but found words inadequate. As he was unable to tell what he saw, he kept saying that it was "something like this or something like that." Seated upon what resembled a throne, surrounded by what seemed to be living creatures (the cherubim), he saw one who had the "likeness as it were of a human form" (1:26). What he saw was "the appearance of the likeness of the glory of the Lord" (1:28).

Strange beings, wheels, and a firmament all a-glitter set the stage for Ezekiel's call. He was given a scroll and told to eat it. He did so, and found that it tasted sweet as honey. Yet he was to say harsh things to a harsh and stubborn people.

God often spoke to his prophet in a seemingly imperious tone. Time and again Ezekiel was addressed as *son of man,* as if he needed to be reminded of his insignificance in the presence of the Almighty.

Isaiah, in contrast to Moses and Jeremiah, was ready and willing to be God's spokesman. Ezekiel, appointed the *watchman* over the house of Israel, became *as hard as flint.* Nothing would stop him from speaking as the Lord wished.

A married man, Ezekiel lived at Tel-abib, near Nippur. Only in 24:16, where he referred to his wife's death, did he manifest his feelings, and that very briefly. Many came to consult and to listen to him as if he were "one who sings love songs with a beautiful voice and plays well on an instrument" (33:32). He was beyond question a strange man who did strange (symbolic) things, once going on a long silent streak.

Ezekiel's exile had begun in 597 BC. The prophet inveighed against idolatrous practices back in Jerusalem. Astarte (an abomination) was honored within the sacred precincts of the Temple, and women wept there for Tammuz, the Babylonian god of vegetation and/or fertility (8:14). The city would fall, he warned, and the glory of God would leave Jerusalem (10:1-23).

Whatever else he was, Ezekiel was intriguing. He pursued one theme—faithless Israel would be punished. The allegory of the vine (16) and that of marriage (16 and 23) contain very strong language. He emphasized God's goodness to his people (20), and then composed the famous *Song of the Sword* (21). Nebuchadnezzar would visit Jerusalem again. Unrealistic dreams of freedom, inspired by Egypt, were doomed to failure. But then (18:22-24) Ezekiel uttered a messianic prophecy (*a shoot*) of restoration under a Davidic dynasty. God has a hand in things....

Jerusalem was in fact destroyed, and the news was disheartening for the exiles in Babylon.

Before the fall of Jerusalem, Ezekiel, like his contemporary Jeremiah, had been very vocal about God's wrath. Once Jerusalem had fallen, however, he assumed the role of comforter. Formerly he relished the idea of divine justice; sinners would get what they deserved. Later (40-48) he would speak of restoration, and would draw up detailed plans for the Temple that was to be built in Jerusalem.

Ezekiel also penned diatribes against the nations. The splendor and lyric qualities of his oracles against Tyre (26-28) rank among the *chef d'oeuvres* of ancient literature. Tyre had conquered the world not by force of arms but by commerce. But Tyre would fall!

Ezekiel's great contribution to religious thought is

his *teaching on retribution, or justice.* The ancients in general tended to think in terms of wholes. In *collective* thinking, the individual was part of a whole, and what one did, all did. All shared in a collective reward (for good) or punishment (for evil done). Before 587 BC, Amos, Hosea, Micah, Isaiah, Zephaniah, and Jeremiah dealt with retribution from a national aspect. Ezekiel described it graphically: "The fathers have eaten sour grapes, and the children's teeth are set on edge" (18:2). Texts like that, and Deuteronomy 5:9, send shivers up one's spine!

Broad terms like race and nation, tribe and family are very useful, but they have to be handled with care. The idea of taking the blame for someone else's crimes goes against the grain. Collective thinking has its drawbacks. It is unfair that those innocent of wrongdoing should be punished for another's crimes. Ezekiel also was of this mind.

In Ezekiel 9, those to be spared punishment were marked with an X. Thanks to a gradual, progressive refinement of the idea of justice, retribution became less and less a collective matter. The Lord said to Ezekiel, "The soul that sins shall die.... If a man is righteous, he shall surely live" (18:5-9). The same view is set forth in 33:1-20.

The Books of Chronicles and Sirach reflect this new doctrine about individual punishment or reward, but the old mentality was hard to dislodge. In New Testament times, the disciples asked Jesus, "Rabbi, who sinned, this man or his parents, that he was born blind?" (Jn 9:2)

Ezekiel, a watchman appointed by God, was also a messenger of comfort and consolation. He passed on the Lord's words about shepherds in a charming allegory which Jesus himself was to use when he spoke about the Good Shepherd (compare John 10 with Ezekiel 34:11+).

Both the land and the people shall be restored (36:25-27). The marvelous *Vision of the Dry Bones* (37:1-28), has been put into unforgettable music. It is an unusually striking promise of the return from exile.

After twenty-five years in exile, Ezekiel looked forward to the great restoration and in three great frescos described a new Temple, a new cult, and a great territorial division (40-43; 44-46; 47-48).

The dimensions of the new Temple are carefully spelled out. Next, the prophet follows an angel to the east gate, and sees the glory of the Lord returning (43:2-5) to the Holy City. Only Zadokite priests will be allowed to serve in this Temple.

Then, the *vidi aquam* (I saw the water). Ezekiel saw a stream flowing from the eastern gate and growing into a mighty flood which would water the desert all the way to the Dead Sea (47:1-12). It would cause trees to grow along its banks, all of them bearing marvelous fruits. Such a vision (40-48) would never be realized literally. Taken symbolically, however, it speaks of God's glorious and majestic Church, whence rivers of grace flow upon and through the world.

Some of the Church Fathers felt that the gate mentioned in Ezekiel 43, through which the God of Israel returned to the Temple, and through which no other was ever to enter or pass (44:1-2), refers to the Virgin Mary. More probably it signifies that the Lord has returned to his Temple permanently, not to depart again.

Second Isaiah and Jubilation

Time marches ever on, and all things change. Even the once mighty neo-Babylonian empire, which produced powerful kings like Nabopolassar (626-605), and Nebuchadnezzar (604-551), was to end. Nabonidus, son of a priestess of the moon goddess Sin, was its last king.

Cyrus the Persian became king of the Medes in 549 BC and by defeating Croesus of Lydia in 547 BC, and Nabonidus in 539, he became supreme lord of Mesopotamia and of Greece as well.

These developments were followed with intense interest by the exiles from Judah. Among them a new voice, belonging to a great but nameless prophet, was raised. It was the voice of one now known as Second Isaiah. In passage after passage, in splendid outbursts of lyric expression, he stirred hope and optimism among the exiles (40-66).

With rhapsodic enthusiasm, this prophet spoke to the exiles of consolation to come. The long exile (586-538) had caused widespread discouragement, but now (probably around 540) there was good news: the exile was to end. It was time to think of preparing a royal road across the desert, of making straight the path of the Lord, who would lead his people back to their homeland. The all-powerful God is to be trusted; he comes to rescue his people Israel. The sheer exuberance of Second Isaiah stirs even modern readers. But there is more to him than that: deep mystery and profound thought, too.

Many times Israel had been thought of as God's servant, but Second Isaiah adds mystery to this concept. Four times, in chapters 42, 49, 50, and 52-53, a special servant of the Lord makes his appearance. He is to liberate his people and be a light to the nations. He will suffer and die, not for his own sins, but for those of all mankind. In the end, even his tomb shall be glorious.

How identify this Servant? This is a complex question. Some Jewish interpreters of Isaiah recognize in the Servant the whole people of Israel so often persecuted; others see a reference to an individual Servant of God.

Christians, on the other hand, have long held that the Servant of the Lord is Jesus Christ, an individual *Messiah*. Like the Servant of Second Isaiah, the sinless Jesus courageously and without complaining, atoned for all and brought healing to sinful humankind.

From a Christian perspective, chapter 53 is a magnificent expression of Jesus' saving act of redemption. It can illumine the unique revelation, found in the Gospel, of God's extraordinary love for his sinful children.

The grandeur and the glory of a new Jerusalem await the returning exiles. The description of this city leaves one gasping. Walls to be built of precious stones! Inside those walls people living in justice and peace! And that is not all. God himself will be the light of the new kingdom, which will need no sun nor moon. The nations will come streaming to Jerusalem, bringing with them all manner of rich gifts.

It is easy to see why Second Isaiah is highly thought of. "Breath-taking" describes him well. Even the casual reader will appreciate the force and beauty of these chapters. Here one will encounter phrases and ideas which Jesus himself noticed and used (cf. 56:7).

Vatican II made its own the stirring words of Second Isaiah 55:1ff.: "Everyone who thirsts, come to the waters; and he who has no money, come, buy and eat...."

Second Isaiah's conception of God is on a par with the most exalted teaching of the Old Testament. His monotheism is explicit, and his words about the greatness and omnipotence of God are unrivalled. He is a peer among peers.

Among his claims to our respect and admiration is his ability to see the hand of God at work in all the events of history. Second Isaiah was a universalist, a man of daring faith. He perceived God as the master of history, and saw the value of vicarious suffering for the sins of men and women of all times.

Haggai, the Temple Builder

The Babylonian exile lasted 49 years, from 587-538 BC. This meant that a whole generation of Jews was exposed to pagan ways of living and thinking. Had not God raised up prophets among the exiles, they would soon have forgotten Jerusalem and their ancestral faith, along with its laws, rules, and sacrifices.

Actually, the exile was a blessing in disguise, strong medicine but also a purifying process. Among other things, Israel learned in exile that God was everywhere, not limited or controlled by an earthly temple or city. One might say that the seeds of universalism, so characteristic of Christianity, were thus being sown. Post-exilic Judaism would be forever different.

Long before the exile, mechanical and meaningless religion had drawn fiery words from the prophet Amos. The trappings of religion, often misdirected to idols, meant nothing at all. Isaiah and Jeremiah had also been severe critics of externalism. "It is obedience I want, not sacrifice, says the Lord" (cf. 1 Sam 15:22).

Still, externals do have their importance. We humans were not given a body for nothing. Human activities such as worship require the participation of the whole person. Kneeling, bowing, singing, praying aloud or silently with others, are all religious acts in and through which the body plays its part in a formal, public acknowledgment of God. History has shown time and again that a merely inward recognition of God cannot keep religion alive.

The "returnees" no doubt comprised the majority of

the exiles, but the numbers given in Chronicles-Ezra-Nehemiah are almost certainly inflated. Some of the exiles were reluctant to just "pull up stakes" and leave for home. Josephus, the Jewish historian, notes that many chose to remain in Babylon. The return probably went on for a number of years.

Once re-settled in their own land, the exiles became aware that something was missing. Houses had needed to be rebuilt, of course, but one could not indefinitely ignore the fact that the Temple lay in ruins, and nothing had been done about it. In 520 BC, the prophet Haggai began to urge Zerubbabel, the governor of Judah, to rebuild the Lord's house. When Cyrus had freed the exiles, he had returned to them the vessels and ornaments that had once adorned the Temple. Time now to rebuild, Haggai said, and to restore the sacred objects to their proper place.

Haggai was clearly an organizer, a man who got things done, a modern CEO. With infectious enthusiasm, he spoke of raising a house of wood and stone that would be a sign of God's presence in the midst of his people. Indeed, it would be a house filled with glory, out-shining the previous Temple.

God's redemptive activity on behalf of his people would be crowned, Haggai argued, by the Lord's making Zerubbabel his *signet ring* (2:23). This odd expression has in fact messianic overtones which deserve some notice.

As long as few people could read or write, documents were notarized, so to speak, by placing a special mark or seal on clay or other material. The seal indicated ownership or intention.

Ancient seals looked very much like a piece of chalk about an inch long, They were bored through lengthwise and worn about the neck. Sometimes seals were engraved *(intaglio)* on semi-precious stones and worn on a ring. Every seal was highly prized by the owner, who guarded it jealously. Haggai spoke of Zerubbabel as the Lord's *signet ring.* It is an unusual expression, but clear enough. This governor, who was of the line of David, and who would see to the restoration of the Temple, was regarded as important and precious in the eyes of the Lord. He was a certified representative of the Lord. Through him the messianic hope would be carried on (Jer 22:24).

Israel's faith, preserved so unpretentiously during the exile, would in the fullness of time find glorious expression in the Christian Church.

Zechariah, the Visionary

Zechariah lived at the same time as Haggai and had two things on his mind: the restoration of the Temple and the spiritual well-being of his people. If Haggai was comfortable with hammer and nails, Zechariah the priest handled the blueprints. Between the two men, the Temple would be restored, and new life infused into messianic hopes.

Eight visions were given to Zechariah one night (1-6). In response to his queries, an angel explained what they meant, but even with angelic aid, these visions remain confusing. There were the four horsemen, horns, and smiths; the measuring line; the high priest; the seven-branched lampstand; the flying scroll; the *ephah* and the woman; the four chariots and in 4:8 and 6:12, the *Branch*, identified with Joshua the high-priest, or with Zerubbabel.

Symbolic language is not always clear, for things keep slipping out of focus. But despite the obscurity, symbolic language, adopted out of political prudence, was a way to convey *comforting words* (1:13) to an often beleaguered community.

The rebuilding of God's House was given top priority by Zerubbabel. As governor, he was actively involved in the project. Once God's house was "taken care of," evil would be driven off. An extraordinary spiritual rejuvenation of the people *and of all peoples* was expected. A new spirit was in the air. One might dream again of messianic expectations. "On the day of small things" (4:10), Zerubbabel, also known as the "Shoot" (6:11-12), would set the capstone in place. The day would then dawn when "many peoples and strong nations shall come to seek the Lord of hosts in Jerusalem" (8:22).

As governor of a land which had shortly before fallen under Persian domination, Zerubbabel held a very important position. In addition he was the son of Shealtiel *of the line of David*. As he went about the rebuilding of the Temple of the Lord in Jerusalem, it may have occurred to Persian observers that a dangerous liaison between Church and state might be in the making. The situation would bear watching, to say the least.

Here then may lie the answer to a textual puzzle found in 3:8. Perhaps it was to allay suspicions of disloyalty to the Persian crown that the name of Joshua the *high-priest* appears in conjunction with "Shoot," whereas in 6:11-13 the "Shoot" is definitely associated with Zerubbabel, the descendant of David who governed Judah!

Zechariah proclaimed that the joys of the messianic age would be great. Not only would Jerusalem be inhabited, but there would be a great harvest of peace. Faithfulness and justice would prevail; men would speak the truth to one another. Honesty and tranquillity would

prevail throughout the land (8:1-17). And many peoples
and strong nations would converge on Jerusalem, there
to implore the favor of the Lord (8:21).

"In those days, ten men from the nations of every
tongue shall take hold of the robe of a Jew, saying, 'Let us
go with you, for we have heard that God is with you'"
(8:23).

With the Lord protecting his city, it will need no
walls, but will be open to the world. In the *Holy Land*
(2:16) there will be peace. (This is the first and only time
in the Bible that Israel is so described.)

In these lines, one can discern the new and exciting
idea of a universal peace under God. There is nothing of
narrow nationalism in Zechariah.

The second part of the Book of Zechariah (9-14) is
different from the first and seems to reflect a later era,
that of Alexander the Great (333 BC). The prevailing tone
is one of violence and confusion, harshness and cruelty.
Apocalyptic imagery occurs, but prophets and prophecy
are only briefly mentioned.

There is, however, a single passage (9:9-10) of rare
beauty and serenity. It is a description of the Messiah to
come, and is familiar to us from its use in Matthew 21:4.

"Rejoice greatly, O daughter of Zion!
Shout aloud, O daughter of Jerusalem!
Lo, your king comes to you;
triumphant and victorious is he,
humble and riding on an ass,
on a colt the foal of an ass."

Renouncing the panoply of kings and mighty men,
the Messiah is to come in humility, riding the traditional
mount of princes, a donkey. No horses or chariots for
him. He will be a prince of peace (cf. also 11:7ff.; 12:10).

The thirty pieces of silver are mentioned in 11:12.

Malachi the Messenger

The Hebrew word *malach* means messenger and the "i" affixed to it means *my*. Who was this prophet whose book closes the Old Testament? Speculation has been unable to answer this question. The Jewish Talmud suggests that he was Ezra; others identify him with Nehemiah or Zerubbabel. His identity remains a mystery.

The prophecy of Malachi—only three short chapters—has to be fitted in somewhere between the years 520 and 450 BC. The glorious return from exile had by no means meant Paradise Regained. Jerusalem had been left in ruins in 586 BC. The first task facing the returnees had been to make the city again habitable. Then, in response to the urgings of Haggai and Zechariah, the rebuilding of the Temple began. By 515 BC, despite several setbacks, and twenty-three years after the return, the Temple was reopened.

Malachi probably lived around 450 BC. He saw all too clearly that from a spiritual point of view, there was much work to be done. Materially speaking, things were bad. The poor were being exploited. Laborers were defrauded of wages, and widows and children of their slender resources. Religious observance too was at a very low ebb. Imperfect animals were being offered to the Lord in sacrifice! Religion had become unimportant.

The policeman's lot is not a happy one, nor is that of a prophet. Both, however, are indispensable to a healthy community.

As we shake our heads over Malachi's description of the situation of religion in Jerusalem, we are reassured to learn that a loving God has his own plans for the future.

"From the rising of the sun to its setting,
my name is great among the nations,
and in every place incense is offered to my name,
and a pure offering" (1:11).

The Council of Trent saw in these words a reference to the universal sacrifice of the Mass, offered daily in churches throughout the world.

In Malachi's day there was need for encouraging words. The old saying, "like the priest, so the people," is ever true. The damage done by a lax and uneducated clergy is beyond measure. In his lively style (always asking questions and answering them), Malachi describes an ideal priest thus:

"True instruction was in his mouth,
and no wrong was found on his lips....
He turned many from iniquity.
For the lips of a priest should guard knowledge,
and men should seek instruction from his mouth,
for he is the messenger of the Lord of hosts" (2:6ff.).

Malachi addressed another issue that was crucial in his day. He spoke about divorce. Wives, it appears, were being taken, used, and discarded at will. Malachi asks husbands to consider this in the light of religious principle (2:14-16): the covenant between man and wife is of divine ordinance. St. Paul (Eph 5:28-33) would heartily applaud Malachi's "I (the Lord) hate divorce."

In chapter 3 Malachi records a lively dialogue between the Lord and "an ordinary man." (There are in this short book no less than seven such exchanges, with eight "rebuttals" *Yet you say....*) Can a man fob God off with imperfect sacrifices, or shortchange him in the matter of tithes? "A book of remembrance was written before him (the Lord) of those who feared the Lord and thought on his name...." On those who fear him, God will "open the windows of heaven for you and pour down for you an overflowing blessing" (3:16, 10).

On judgment day the Lord will enter his Temple, purify the sons of Levi, and establish justice.

"Behold, I send my messenger
to prepare the way before me" (3:1).

Who was this messenger? Malachi answers (4:5):

"Behold, I will send you Elijah the prophet
before the great and terrible day of the Lord comes."

Jesus declared that this prophecy was fulfilled in the coming of John the Baptist (Mt 11:14).

The preaching of Micah and Isaiah prepared the way for the great religious reform of Hezekiah. The preaching of Malachi led to the reform of Ezra-Nehemiah, which would come later.

Breached many times, the walls of Jerusalem had lain in ruin for decades. Yet to raise them up, in what was now a Persian satrapy in West-of-Euphrates, was an undertaking that could easily be interpreted as a dangerous assertion of independence. When Xerxes, Darius' successor, had learned of the rebuilding of the walls back in 520 BC, he had ordered the work halted.

Jerusalem thus remained a defenseless city until the arrival in 444 BC of Nehemiah, cup-bearer to Artaxerxes. Work on the walls was begun at once. The opposition of the Samaritans and Ammonites was so determined that the builders of the wall were forced to work, as Nehemiah put it (4:11), with a trowel in one hand and a sword in the other. But in 52 days, the job was done and Jerusalem could once again relax behind walls.

Another notable event during this period was Ezra's great reform. All who had married alien (non-Jewish women) were given an ultimatum: either dismiss your wives and children, or leave and take them with you.

This drastic step was taken to insure religious unity. Harsh as it was, the measure produced a Jewish community able to resist the siren voices of Hellenism, which would soon be upon them.

Obadiah the Fierce

The Book of Obadiah—the name means slave or servant of the Lord—is the shortest of the prophetical books. The 21 verses have been thoroughly examined and discussed, but their date of composition is uncertain, with possibilities ranging from the 9th to the 4th century BC. Two passages (1-4 and 5) are almost identical with Jeremiah 49:14-16 and 49:9; if it was Obadiah who did the borrowing, this would date him about 587 BC.

Obadiah's brief prophecy deals with two things: the *punishment of Edom*, and the *Day of the Lord*.

The land of Edom extended from the Dead Sea to the gulf of Aqaba. Lofty Mt. Sela overlooked the capital of Edom, Petra, "the rose-red city, half as old as time." It was (and still is) reached by a deep, twisting gorge which eventually opens upon a scene of great beauty—a great basin, 1,000 yards wide, featuring facades and columns carved in colored rock. It is easily one of the most spectacular sights in the Near East.

Obadiah declares, in language vigorous, poetic and even fierce, that Edom will be punished. The Edomites, descendants of Esau, will pay for their refusal to allow the Israelites to pass through their territory when going from Egypt (Num 20:14-21). On the Day of the Lord, Jacob/Israel shall be exalted, and Mt. Zion shall be glorious. "Kingship shall be the Lord's."

Joel, Penance and Pentecost

The Book of Joel, listed second among the twelve minor prophets, probably dates from around 400 BC. Apocalyptic and eschatological in tone, this book was occasioned by a devastating plague of locusts in which the prophet saw God's punishment. The daily sacrifices had been halted, and acknowledgment of the sins which separated the people from God was an urgent necessity.

Looking straight at a grasshopper, one can easily see that its head resembles that of a horse. With only a bit more imagination one can imagine the legs to be spears, held upright by a Don Quixote ready to joust with a windmill.

Joel (2:4) noted this likeness. In his vivid description one can almost hear the clattering of horses' hooves and the rumbling of chariot wheels. Nothing could halt the locusts. They scaled the walls and climbed through doors and windows, leaving destruction and ruin in their awful wake.

Small wonder, then, that Joel's thoughts twice turned to the *Day of the Lord* (1:15; 2:11), a day of darkness and gloom, exceedingly terrible. These ominous words were in fact an invitation to turn to the Lord. Time indeed to do penance for sins, Joel says, time to "rend your hearts and not your garments. Return to the Lord, your God" (2:12ff.). He is good and merciful. He will take pity. Good times will come again.

The prophets, all men of deep religious conviction, hated superficiality. Gazing over the passing scene, they saw the shallowness of the religious observances of their day. Ritual easily becomes mechanical and empty of meaning. It has, alas, always been more difficult to rend one's heart than one's garments. Like the prophets who preceded him, Joel knew full well the worthlessness of acts of worship that did not reflect the inner sentiments of the worshipper.

Beginning with Amos, Hebrew religious thought was dominated by the idea of the *Day of the Lord, Judgment Day*. Where shall it occur? Only in Joel 3:2 and 12 is the Valley of Jehoshaphat mentioned in the Bible. According to popular belief, the last judgment will take place near the junction of the valley of GeHinnom with Kidron valley. The hills overlooking this area are literally covered with tombs (still white-washed each spring). Who could ask for a better seat from which to watch the General Judgment!

Meanwhile, much remains to be done. Now is a time, Joel declares, for prayer and fasting. Now one should pray with the priests: "Spare, O Lord, your people. Make not your heritage a reproach" (cf. 2:17). Now more than ever the forces of evil must be fought against. Turning Isaiah's phrase around (Is 2:4), Joel pictures God's soldiers as beating "ploughshares into swords, and...pruning hooks into spears" (3:10). Even the weak man shall say, "I am a warrior." There is a battle to be won.

But there is more. Joel is also the prophet of Pentecost (2:28ff.).

"I will pour out my spirit on all flesh;
your sons and your daughters shall prophesy,
your old men shall dream dreams,
and your young men shall see visions.
Even upon the men servants and maidservants
in those days, I will pour out my spirit."

In his impromptu sermon on the first Pentecost Sunday, (Acts 2:17-21), St. Peter declared to his hearers that the promise of the Holy Spirit was being fulfilled before their eyes.

Daniel and Apocalyptic Visions

Daniel is a most intriguing book. In Roman Catholic bibles it is the last of the major prophets. In the Jewish scriptures it appears among the "writings" which close the Old Testament. The book comes to us in various languages. It begins in Hebrew (1-2:4), switches to Aramaic (2:4b-7:28), goes back to Hebrew (8-12), and ends in Greek. Chapters 13-14 are found only in Greek and Latin versions.

The opening stories are set in Babylon and suggest exilic times (587-538 BC), but the book was probably written much later. The visions in chapters 9-12, using apocalyptic imagery, touch on events of the Persian, Greek, and Seleucid periods up to Antiochus IV Epiphanes (175-164 BC), a king who attempted to force Jews to worship a statue set up by him in the Temple. This was the last straw. Led by the Maccabees, the Jews revolted, and after three years (168-165 BC) were victorious.

The Book of Daniel exemplifies a kind of literature that was written for the express purpose of encouraging people undergoing some kind of crisis. It was designed to strengthen their confidence in God. Stories like Daniel in the lions' den, or Shadrach, Meshach, and Abednego in the fiery furnace, or the handwriting on the wall, all make the same point: God is always in control and will establish his kingdom.

How this triumph was to be realized was seen in visions. Mysterious beasts, a lion, a bear, a leopard, and "the beast," appear (7:1+). In 7:9-10, *the Ancient One* is seen seated upon a throne, and in 7:13-15, a *son of man* comes upon the clouds of heaven to receive from the Ancient One an everlasting kingship. After a brief reign of three and a half years, the fourth beast is deprived of all its power. Chapter 9:24-27, tells of the *seventy weeks* that shall precede the destruction of the *horrible abomination*.

None of this would make sense to someone lacking a knowledge of history. The beasts stand for various kingdoms: Babylon, the Medes and Persians, Greece, and then the Seleucids and Ptolemies.

The *Ancient One* who dispenses justice from a throne of fire is clearly meant to be God. To see the beast slain and thrown into the fire, assures the reader that any power opposed to God will be overthrown.

Son of man is a title Jesus often used of himself. The son of man spoken of by Daniel was to come upon the clouds (which in the Bible symbolize the presence of God) to receive extraordinary authority from the Ancient One. Who was this Son of Man?

Symbols are by nature imprecise and difficult to pin down. The Son of Man may signify the "saints" who are to receive an eternal kingdom, or the Chosen People, who are one day to form a messianic kingdom with the Messiah as their king.

With Matthew 8:20, 24:30, and 26:64 in mind, Christians can argue that Jesus interpreted the texts about the Son of Man in a very personal way, of himself. In his human nature he was aware of his destiny—death through humiliation, and then glory. His Church, the Christian community, shares in his destiny.

Valuable theological points are contained in the concluding chapters, such as the doctrine of the angels and (12:2) the resurrection of the body (see also 2 Macc 7:9). Chapters 13-14 are considered later additions. The story of Susanna (13) proves Daniel's shrewdness, and illustrates the power of prayer. Chapter 14 is a satire on idolatry.

Daniel 3:33; 4:2; 7:14 speaks of the coming of the kingdom. This will be the central theme of the Synoptic Gospels. The Book of Daniel is mature apocalyptic; it has its counterpart in the New Testament Book of Revelation.

Jonah, Peevish Prophet

Jonah is one of the best known characters in the Bible. He is listed among the minor prophets, but his book is in a class all by itself. It tells a story in the third person singular, capturing the reader's attention from the very first line. The tale highlights a profound theological truth and subtly insinuates a very important point—that God's ways are not the same as ours.

Jonah is described as the son of Amittai. A man of that name had lived during the reign of Jeroboam II (766-746 BC), but it was a later, unknown author who attributed this book to him. It is not improbable that Jonah was the last book of the Old Testament to be written.

The action begins at once. God orders Jonah to go to Nineveh, the capitol of Assyria, the ancient archetype of evil. Jonah is not at all pleased with his assignment, so he books passage on a ship headed in the opposite direction. A storm arises. Realizing that he is the reason for it, Jonah heroically advises the pagan crew to throw him into the sea, which they do. He is promptly swallowed by a huge fish prepared for that purpose by the Lord. Three days later, spewed forth upon the shore, the reluctant prophet makes his way to Nineveh.

The book's description of Nineveh is greatly exaggerated. The excavated ruins of the city rule out the city's enormous size. The grandeur attributed to it is a storyteller's windowdressing. The real point of the story is that God's plan does not overlook even the most wicked of peoples.

To some Jews of that time, such an idea would have been simply unthinkable. They would have scoffed at so democratic an idea. The exclusivism of the prevailing attitude resembled that exaggerated nationalism we may hear voiced in such slogans as: "My country, right or wrong, my country."

The story of Jonah rejects a narrow outlook. God's mercy cannot be measured by human standards, nor limited by geography, time, or a particular tradition. Divine mercy is like God himself, something beyond measuring or understanding.

Jonah preached penance and repentance as per instructions, but his heart was not in it. He was irritated by the fact that not only the king, but even the animals in Nineveh did penance. Nineveh was spared destruction! "Do you do well to be angry?" God asked, quietly.

Next, the plant under whose shade Jonah had planned to sit watching fire and brimstone rain down on the city, shriveled and died! Faint under the sun, Jonah felt angry enough to die. But once again the Lord reproved his selfish prophet, upset over a plant, by asking softly: "Should not I pity Nineveh, that great city?"

So ends the story. Jonah is a narrow-minded, peevish man. Yet God is kind to him, as he is to everyone. God is disposed to show love and mercy, whether to Jew or to non-Jew, especially if anyone does penance and implores his forgiveness.

How consoling to learn that God's ways are not our ways, that he is ever ready to intervene and show mercy, both to our enemies and to us, provided we are not selfish.

Who has not wondered, on reading this humorous little tale, what it would be like to spend some time in the belly of a whale? What to do? In chapter 2 Jonah composes a splendid poem which does justice to a unique situation. Even more than that, it is a joyful hymn to the glory of God, from whom alone comes deliverance.

4. Select Messianic Prophecies

Genesis 3:15

> "I will put enmity between you and the woman,
> and between your seed and her seed;
> He shall bruise your head
> while you shall bruise his heel."

The setting is the Garden of Eden. God has just elicited an admission of guilt from Adam and Eve, who tried lamely to shift the blame for their sin to someone else.

God then announced that from this moment on, a state of radical opposition, a kind of war, would exist between *the* woman and the serpent, and their respective progeny. There would be an ongoing war between them, the woman's offspring striking (stamping on) the serpent's head, and the serpent striking back at the off-spring of the woman.

These words clearly mean that in the end, good will be victorious over evil. The choice of a serpent to symbolize the devil (or powers of evil) reflects our instinctive feelings of revulsion toward snakes. In a contest between a man standing upright and a snake, the outcome is known in advance.

This passage promises the coming of the Redeemer. As the seed of the woman, he will crush the serpent's head. Thus Genesis 3:15, with its message of Good News, can rightfully be called the *protoevangelium*, the "first Gospel."

In the Latin Vulgate version, Genesis 3:15 reads: *Ipsa* (she) *conteret caput tuum* (shall crush thy head). The Promised One and his Mother appear together, for the text continues with: "And he...." Both the child and his mother, then, have important roles to play in the work of restoration/redemption.

Thus artfully are we introduced to the first messianic prophecy. Stated well in advance is the coming of him who will be triumphant over sin. God's plan, sabotaged at the beginning, will be restored in an unexpected but glorious fashion by Jesus, the Son of God and of Mary.

Messianic texts deal with the Messiah. That word implies an anointing with oil whereby one is "set apart" and recognized as having special prerogatives and powers. Kings were anointed for that reason, and the Messiah to come was to be a king, concerned with right and justice.

Stroke by stroke, a picture is painted of the Messiah. He will be born of a woman, and will be victorious over the great enemy of his people. Glory, then, is to be his, and strength.

Genesis 49:10-11

"The scepter shall not depart from Judah,
nor the ruler's staff from between his feet,
until he comes to whom it belongs;
and to him shall be the obedience of the peoples."

One of Jacob's blessings, this text speaks of the supremacy of the tribe of Judah. In every age, kings were recognized as persons of authority. This was symbolized by the mace he held between his legs as he sat dispensing justice.

Here is a veiled prophecy about a king of Judah who would rule over the nations. Somewhat obscurely, the oracle suggests King David. There next appear these mysterious words:

"Binding his foal to the vine
and his ass's colt to the choice vine,
he washes his garments in wine
and his vesture in the blood of grapes."

Numbers 24:17

"I see him, but not now
I behold him, but not nigh:
A star shall come forth out of Jacob,
And a scepter shall rise out of Israel."

Balaam was a soothsayer who had been hired by the king of Moab to put a curse on the approaching Israelites. He was not able to do so; instead, blessings issued from his mouth. The above lines are from his fourth oracle, and seem to refer to a descendant of the patriarch Jacob.

The One to come, Balaam says, will be like a *star*. Balaam was acquainted with the blazing stars of the desert night. He who was to come would know splendor, and would rule over Israel. All is not clear here. Prophecy is not mathematics, nor a jig-saw puzzle that yields to persistence. Prophecy has a wide range, and is directed sometimes at an individual person, the Messiah himself, or sometimes at various aspects of what we call messianic times.

Balaam's words are not quoted in the New Testament, not even in connection with the star of the Magi. However, many of the ancient Fathers considered this passage a messianic prophecy. The Messiah will be brilliant, and will have authority as well.

2 Samuel 7:8, 12, 16

"Thus you shall say to my servant David....
'I will raise up your offspring after you...
and I will establish his kingdom....
Your house and your kingdom shall be made sure
for ever before me;
your throne shall be established forever.'"

This prophecy, in conjunction with others like Psalm 132:10-18, which mentions David as the Lord's *anointed*, and a *sprout* that would shoot forth, is the basis for Jewish expectation of a Messiah, the son of David. (See Acts 2:30.)

Amos 5:15, 18

"Hate evil, and love good
and establish justice in the gate;
it may be that the Lord, the God of hosts,
will be gracious to the remnant of Joseph....

Woe to you who desire the day of the Lord!"

Amos was the first prophet to speak of the mysterious *Day of the Lord*. It was to be an event that lay in the future. Amos stressed the inevitability of God's justice. There shall be no escaping it. Yet God has another side: he is also merciful. His justice may be fierce, yet he will have pity on a *remnant*.

Promises of glory are one thing, but present reality can be disheartening. Devout God-fearing people endure painful trials, and history shows that saints too suffer. Amos is careful to point out that great trials, sufferings, and even death shall not thwart God's plans for the world. Nor does God need any help in carrying out his plan. He who created all things out of nothing will, however, graciously make use of a tiny remnant.

Amos 9:11-15

"'In that day I will raise up the booth of David that is fallen....
That they may possess the remnant of Edom
and all the nations who are called by my name....
Behold, the days are coming,' says the Lord,
'when the plowman shall overtake the reaper
and the treader of grapes, him who sows the seed;
the mountains shall drip sweet wine,
and all the hills shall flow with it.'"

There are two items here. The first is in reference to the gentiles. In Acts 15:15, James cites this text as justifying the apostolic decision to preach to the pagans.

Secondly, there is a description of an extraordinary joy that will attend the Day of the Lord. So pervasive will be the peace and happiness of that day that it can only be dealt with by the use of hyperbole. Imagine a vine or land so fertile that harvest-time would immediately follow the sowing of the seed, and vintage-time the planting of the vines.

Nothing like this has ever happened in the material order, but the messianic times are something else. Through the sacraments of the Church, one enters into a union with God that surpasses anything even Amos imagined.

Cf. Isaiah 7:14

> "The virgin shall be with child and bear a son,
> and shall call him Emmanuel."

The Church has always seen this text fulfilled in the birth of Christ, which took place 700 years later. How then could it be a sign to the House of Israel? Isaiah, who may not have seen this clearly, probably had the king's wife, the future mother of Hezekiah, in mind. That particular birth from a young wife thus constituted a *type* of something even more extraordinary, namely, of the birth of God's Son, Jesus, from his mother, the Virgin Mary. Hezekiah became one of the good kings, but Jesus was truly Emmanuel, or God with us.

A biblical *sign* could be an event which had meaning because it was foretold or had been asked for (Gen 24:14; 1 Sam 10:2). Or it could be something clearly miraculous, as here: "A virgin (*'almah*) shall conceive and bear a son...Emmanuel."

The Hebrew word for "virgin" is *'almah*. Another word for virgin, *bethulah*, could refer to even an old woman, whereas *'almah* definitely implied a young woman who was unmarried or marriageable. The term was not used of a woman wrongfully pregnant. It is interesting that Isaiah used the definite pronoun "the." This *'almah* was very special.

Catholics hold that the Blessed Virgin Mary was the fulfillment of Isaiah's prophecy, and that she was special because she was at once both virgin and mother of Jesus, the Savior.

Also unusual is the fact that she, not the father, would *name* this child. The name she was to impose upon him would indicate who and what this child was. He would be *Emmanuel*, that is, "*God with us*."

Analysis

Is Isaiah 7:10-14 a genuine prophecy? It has been given much attention and many different explanations:

1) There is nothing messianic here at all. Ahaz was a young man recently married, and Isaiah was probably referring to Ahaz's son, Hezekiah. Still, Ahaz' wife could hardly have been called an *'almah*. The term does not apply to married women.

2) The *'almah* was Isaiah's wife. But the prophet could hardly have called her "the virgin." She bore him two sons, but their names could not have signified Emmanuel, God with us.

3) A modern view is that Isaiah was referring to *any* male child who would shortly be born. Again, such a view fails to do adequate justice to "the virgin."

4) The prophecy is to be taken literally. The virgin who becomes pregnant and bears a son while remaining a virgin is the Blessed Virgin Mary. The Septuagint (Greek version of the Old Testament) uses the word *parthenos* (i.e., virgin) in Isaiah 7:14. The prophet Micah (5:2) echoes Isaiah when he speaks of *a special woman* who would give birth in Bethlehem.

Isaiah 9:2

"The people who walked in darkness
have seen a great light."

This vague text can hardly be considered a great messianic prophecy, but Christian liturgy and tradition have accommodated it to Christ, who is the Light of the World.

Isaiah 9:6

"To us a child is born, to us a son is given;
and the government will be upon his shoulder,
and his name will be called
Wonderful Counselor, Mighty God,
Everlasting Father, Prince of Peace."

The child spoken of in 7:14 is, as the liturgy and tradition understand it, Christ. A Prince of Peace, he deserves highest praise: he has the wisdom of Solomon, the valor of David, and all the virtues of Moses and the patriarchs. Emmanuel = "God-with-us."

Isaiah 11:1-3

"There shall come forth a shoot from
the stump of Jesse....
And the Spirit of the Lord shall rest upon him,
the spirit of wisdom and understanding,
the spirit of counsel and might,
the spirit of knowledge and the fear of the Lord.
And his delight shall be in the fear of the Lord."

Here we have a fine poem extolling the virtues of the Messiah, who will be of Davidic stock (Jesse was

David's father). The Messiah will be endowed with the Lord's Spirit and shall manifest in his person the virtues of his famous ancestors—David, Solomon, and Jacob—namely, wisdom, prudence, knowledge, and fear of the Lord.

A dead stump conveys the idea of death; a tree has fallen. Then, contrary to all indications, a shoot full of life shall appear on something that was apparently dead. During the Babylonian captivity, the once great kingdom of David had all but disappeared. Now a remarkable messianic king was to appear, as a twig sprouts from a dead stump.

Isaiah 42:1-4

"Behold my servant, whom I uphold,
my chosen, in whom my soul delights;
I have put my spirit upon him,
he will bring forth justice to the nations.
He will not cry or lift up his voice,
or make it heard in the street;
a bruised reed he will not break,
and a dimly burning wick he will not quench....
Till he has established justice in the earth;
and the coastlands wait for his law."

In this first of the four "Servant Songs" Christian tradition sees Christ, Savior also of the coastlands (the gentiles).

Isaiah 49:1-7

"Listen to me, O coastlands, and hearken, you peoples from afar.

The Lord called me from the womb,
from the body of my mother he named my name.
He made my mouth like a sharp sword,
in the shadow of his hand he hid me;
he made me a polished arrow,
in his quiver he hid me away.
And he said to me, 'You are my servant,
Israel, in whom I will be glorified.'
But I said, 'I have labored in vain
I have spent my strength for nothing and vanity;
yet surely my right is with the Lord,
and my recompense with my God.'"

In this second of the four Servant Songs, the Servant
is described as approved for a special office, ready and
willing to do the Lord's will. The identification of the
Servant with Israel may be a gloss, for verse 5 distin-
guishes him from the people he represents. His task is
seen as the conversion of the world (v. 6).

Isaiah 50:4-11

"The Lord God has given me the tongue of those
who are taught,
that I may know how to sustain with a word
him that is weary.
Morning by morning he wakens,
he wakens my ear....
And I was not rebellious, I turned not backward.
I gave my back to the smiters,
and my cheeks to those who pulled out the beard;
I hid not my face from shame and spitting.
For the Lord God helps me;
therefore I have not been confounded;
therefore I have set my face like a flint,

and I know that I shall not be put to shame;
he who vindicates me is near.
Who will contend with me?
Let us stand up together.
Who is my adversary? Let him come near to me.
Behold, the Lord God helps me;
who will declare me guilty?
Behold, all of them will wear out like a garment;
The moth will eat them up.
Who among you fears the Lord
and obeys the voice of his servant,
and walks in darkness and has no light,
yet trusts in the name of the Lord
and relies upon his God?
Behold, all you who kindle a fire,
and set brands alight!
Walk by the light of your fire,
and by the brands which you have kindled!
This shall you have from my hand:
you shall lie down in torment."

The people do not follow the obedient Servant of the
Lord, and are reproved for this. The Servant willingly
submits to insults and pain, as his vocation demands.
The description of his sufferings resembles that of the
following (fourth) song.

Isaiah 52:13-53:12

The sinless Servant willingly takes upon himself the
sins of his people, thus saving them from divine punishment. Only in Jesus Christ is this prophecy (sometimes
called the "Fifth" Gospel) fulfilled. The idea of his suffering for *others'* sins is something almost incomprehen-

sible. Expiation like this, however appealing to sinners, was new to the ancient and pagan world.

Micah 5:1-4

"But you, O Bethlehem Ephrathah,
who are little to be among the clans of Judah,
from you shall come forth for me
one who is to be ruler in Israel,
whose origin is from of old, from ancient days.
Therefore he shall give them up until the time
when she who is in travail has brought forth."

David was born to an Ephrathite family in Bethlehem (1 Sam 16). He was the youngest of Jesse's sons, and was anointed king there by the prophet Samuel. Micah mentions the mother of the Messiah, thinking perhaps of the *'almah* Isaiah had spoken of some years earlier. Mary and Joseph may have been natives of Bethlehem who moved to Galilee because of the unsettled conditions under Herod.

Jeremiah 31:31-33

"Behold, the days are coming, says the Lord,
when I will make a new covenant
with the house of Israel and the house of Judah....
This is the covenant which I will make
with the house of Israel after those days,
says the Lord:
I will place my law within them
and write it upon their hearts;
and I will be their God,
and they shall be my people."

The *old covenant* made with Moses involved the slaughter of animals, and blood; its terms were spelled out in the ten commandments and graven upon stone.

As he viewed the destruction of the Holy City and its Temple, and the deportation of Jerusalem's citizens to Babylon, Jeremiah spoke of a *new covenant* which was to come. It would mark a new and spiritual relationship between God and his people. It would not be something carved upon stone, but a spiritual kind of union that would exist between every individual and God.

Christians feel that this new covenant was made by Christ at the Last Supper and sealed with his blood on Calvary (Lk 22:20 and 1 Cor 11:25).

Zephaniah 1:14-15

"The great day of the Lord is near....
A day of wrath is that day,
a day of distress and anguish
a day of ruin and devastation,
a day of darkness and gloom,
a day of clouds and thick darkness."

Zephaniah 3:12-13

"I will leave in the midst of you
a people humble and lowly.
They shall seek refuge in the name of the Lord,
those who are left in Israel."

Habakkuk 3:17-19

This is a wonderful protestation of confidence and trust in God, and characteristic of the prophets.

Ezekiel 18:2

"The fathers have eaten sour grapes,
and the children's teeth are set on edge."

This ancient proverb voices the widespread view that retribution was collective, that is, children had to suffer and pay for the sins of their family, clan, or tribe. The Bible is full of such stories. Jeremiah (31:29) and Ezekiel (18:2) broke the mold, so to speak, by speaking of individual responsibility.

The idea of individual retribution would eventually win the day, but slowly (cf. Jn 8:33). Ezekiel promulgated the idea of *individual retribution*. Justice would prevail. Men and women would be rewarded or punished as their deeds deserved.

Ezekiel 33:20

"O house of Israel,
I will judge each of you according to his ways."

Ezekiel 34:11-23
The Good Shepherd

"For thus says the Lord God:
Behold, I, I myself will search for my sheep,
and I will seek them out....
I will rescue them...
bring them out...gather them...feed them....
And I will set up over them one shepherd,
my servant David."

Ezekiel 37:1-14
The dry bones will rise again

Ezekiel 40-48
The new theocracy\a grand idea

Daniel 9:24-27
Seventy weeks of years are decreed....

"From the going forth of the word
Jerusalem to restore and build
to the coming of an anointed one, a prince,
there shall be seven weeks.
Then for sixty-two weeks it shall be built again....
And after the sixty-two weeks, an anointed one
shall be cut off....
And he shall make a strong covenant with many
for one week;
and for half of the week he shall cause sacrifice
and offering to cease;
and upon the wing of abominations shall come
one who makes desolate,
until the decreed end is poured out on
the desolation."

In 605 BC Jeremiah predicted that the coming captivity would last for seventy years (26:11 and 29:10). This round number suggested only that the present generation would die out in exile. While Daniel pondered this, the angel Gabriel explained (9:24-27) that after seventy weeks (of years), the troubles of Daniel's day would end.

This time was divided into periods of varying lengths: 7, 62, and 1 week, which indicate relative proportions of the time that would elapse.

The return from Babylon took place after 49 years of exile (587-538 BC). This corresponds to the seven weeks. It is quite another matter, however, to handle the 62 weeks (= 434 years). No matter what it is subtracted from— whether 605 or 596 or 587 or 538 (all key dates)—no light is gained from the process. The 62/434 represents, then, an indefinite period between the seven weeks and the one week.

The influence of Greece upon the rest of the world can hardly be over-estimated. Everywhere, Greek ways of thinking and living were adopted. But Daniel was assured that this painful period, however long it might last, would also end.

Once the 62 weeks had elapsed, there remained one week. In the first half of that week *an Anointed* one (9:25) was to be cut down. (Onias III, a high priest, actually was murdered in 171 BC.) Half a week later, in 168 BC, the *abomination of desolation,* an image of Jupiter Olympus, was set up in the Temple. It was the spark that ignited the Maccabean Revolt (168-165 BC).

Thus the seven weeks and the one week can be accounted for, more or less. The 62 weeks, or 434 years, probably mean only "a long time," after which the Temple would be cleansed.

Some early Fathers saw in the "anointed one" (9:26) a reference to Jesus and his crucifixion; others held that the last week referred to the end of time.

Haggai 3:23

"On that day, says the Lord of hosts,
I will take you, O Zerubbabel....
And make you like a *signet ring*;
for I have chosen you, says the Lord of hosts."

Zechariah 3:8

"I will bring my servant, the *Branch* (Shoot)."

Zechariah 9:9

"Lo, your king comes to you;
triumphant and victorious is he,
humble and riding on an ass,
on a colt the foal of an ass."

Malachi 1:11

"From the rising of the sun to its setting
my name is great among the nations,
and in every place incense is offered to my name,
and a pure offering."

Joel 2:28-29

"It shall come to pass afterward,
that I will pour out my spirit on all flesh;
your sons and your daughters shall prophesy,
your old men shall dream dreams,
and your young men shall see visions.
Even upon the menservants and the maidservants
in those days, I will pour out my spirit."

5. The Consummation of Prophecy

The Bible speaks of spiritual matters in graphic and concrete fashion, and so did Jesus. His brilliant imagery caused, and still causes, people to marvel. "Where did he learn all this? No one has ever spoken like this!" Yet he spoke of homely things like sowing, reaping, work, sheep, and bread-making.

During the Sermon on the Mount, Jesus spoke directly about himself. His startled listeners heard him say: "Think not that I have come to abolish the law and the prophets; I have come...to fulfill them" (Mt 5:17). He thus declared himself to be the climax, the supreme realization of the promises made by God to the Chosen People. One had only to look at him to learn what God had had in mind from the beginning of creation.

Jesus never backed away from this claim. He was the Light. No longer would people have to wrestle with obscure, fragmentary hints about their origins and destinies. Now they would know about God more clearly. "He who sees me sees the Father."

"In the Old Testament," St. Augustine perceived, "the New lies concealed; in the New, the Old lies revealed." His words draw attention to the marvelous unity and harmony that exists between the two Testaments.

The Law of Moses was clearly superior to any other law the world had known. In Israel alone was place made for the existence and nature of God. Israel alone could boast of the ten commandments and a law that was consonant with a high moral code.

Jesus' words were a claim to a unique and special place in God's plan for the world. His knowledge of who he was and of the role he was to play in life, lay behind his assertion that in himself and in his person a dazzling light was being directed upon the old law and the prophets.

How could such a claim be proven? Jesus made no attempt to cite all the prophetic passages which had spoken of him. He did say, in a synagogue sermon in Nazareth, "Today this scripture (of Isaiah) has been fulfilled in your hearing" (Lk 4:16-22), but only once, when he rode into Jerusalem seated upon a lowly donkey (Zech 9:9), did he act out a prophecy. He was no scissors-and-paste Messiah, limited to collating texts.

The fulfillment to which Jesus referred went beyond anything anyone had ever imagined, hoped for, or hinted at in the Old Testament (1 Cor 2:9; Heb 1:1). He was Emmanuel, or God with us, come into the world in human flesh.

The Gospels speak to us of a Jesus who was buoyantly alive and perfectly human. He surpassed all the eloquent, talented, courageous and pious saints of the Old Testament. No other orator so spoke of spiritual truths and of God, as to draw thousands of people out of the cities and into the desert.

The Bible enjoys a remarkable unity, for the two Testaments are complementary, as Augustine said. Truths proclaimed in the New Testament can be found at least in germ in the Old. The promises of the Old Testament, once expressed in ways that were vague and partial, were to be clearly realized in the person of Jesus.

As ancient obscurities come into focus on Jesus, the shadows retreat. Jesus is beyond question the most famous person the world has ever known. His claim to be the fulfillment of both the Law and the Prophets meant that he considered himself the realization of the divine promises. An astonishing claim!

It is impossible for us to know exactly what Jesus Christ looked like, but it can safely be said that he once lived, did extraordinary things, and rose from the dead. After two thousand years his words and deeds are still known, loved, and remembered. History acknowledges his importance by dating events as having happened before or after him (BC or AD).

Returned from the Babylonian captivity, the Chosen People found that life was harsh and difficult. They also found, however, that there was things worth living for. The promises of glory which filled the Old Testament had never been revoked. The very memory of them would keep hope alive. And one day....

When John the Baptizer, the last of the Old Testament prophets, made his appearance, he pointed his finger at Jesus and said: "Behold, the Lamb of God" (Jn 1:29). The Promised One, the fulfillment of ancient prophecies, the future king and provider of peace and justice, had arrived. It was the time of Jesus the Son of God. Isaac had once asked, "Father, where is the lamb for a burnt offering?" (Gen 22:7) That question was now fully answered.

In speaking of Jesus, St. Peter informed the household of Cornelius: "To him all the prophets bear witness..." (Acts 10:43). The apostle's words were a profound theological witness to the meaning of Jesus' redemptive death and resurrection. The newly-born Christian community would actively pursue and develop this faith.

As we follow Jesus in his public ministry and listen to his words, we become aware that in him the prophets' passion for truth, justice, etc., were everywhere greatly deepened and spiritualized. As we leaf through the prophets, we realize that Jesus gathers their best points together, refining, embellishing, and transcending them.

Amos was an ardent champion of justice and right. Hosea was a man known for his words on love. Micah, a man of the land, was deeply aware of its beauty and of its darker (human) side. Like Amos he was obsessed with the idea of a judgment, and of the vindication of the remnant of Israel on the Day of the Lord. The great Isaiah, observing the frailties of human nature, its posturings and its posing, was alive to God's plan for the future.

The prophet Jeremiah was a man who wrestled with God, and generations of readers have found his inner turmoil much like their own. His struggles were by no means external only. In this prophet we learn of an intense inner life with God, real and powerful. He suffered much and deeply, yet somehow mustered up the courage to struggle against the ungodly. He was the first of the prophets to mention a new covenant, and like Ezekiel, to bring up the matter of individual answerability for things done.

Second Isaiah (chapters 40-66) spoke touchingly of a special Servant of the Lord, who would suffer an ignominious death in expiation for the sins of mankind. He also spoke triumphantly about the return from captivity, a joyous event in which nature itself would take part.

Malachi predicted a marvelous worldwide daily sacrifice, strikingly comparable to that of the Mass. Joel would speak of the coming of the Holy Spirit. A more somber note, one of death and destruction, and even of a revenge consonant with divine justice, was sounded by Nahum and Obadiah. Zechariah (9:9) records the entry of a king and savior into Jerusalem, riding upon a donkey.

The notion of king is one of great complexity. Jesus had no ambitions as an earthly king; his kingdom would be spiritual. The perception of a kingdom that would be universal in scope and beyond the confines of space and time, began to be understood and preached. Jesus, a king both loved and adored, was to reign over a spiritual kingdom open to all nations. This kingdom would be marked by peace and justice. A present reality, it was to have a glorious future as well. Its subjects would be a cross-section of humanity, some good, some bad. The idea of a Church, a spiritual kingdom containing a variety of people from all nations, comes readily to mind.

Together with the rest of the Old Testament, the prophets were part of God's gradual self-disclosure. God adapted himself to various mentalities and stages of human understanding. On the occasion of Jesus' presentation in the Temple, old Simeon declared himself ready to die; he had seen it all: "My eyes have witnessed your saving deed displayed for all the peoples to see" (cf. Lk 2:29). Indeed, in Jesus the dreams and visions of the prophets, carried to new heights, are realized. Jesus' law of love exhausts the teaching of all the Law and the Prophets.

In sum, then, let it be said that the range and sphere of Jesus' kingdom spiritualized and expanded the notion of kingdom beyond the confines of the Old Testament. This is not surprising, for in Christ the prophetic texts take on a deeper meaning. In any case, the historical setting of the old prophecies was both temporal and accidental. The truths they expressed do not change. And the Spirit will guide us into all truth. We have Jesus' word for it.

6. Food for Thought

Isaiah

Is 1:18
Though your sins be like scarlet/crimson...become white as snow/wool

Is 2:4
They shall beat their swords into plowshares

Is 5:1+
The vineyard song

Is 6
ISAIAH'S CALL

Is 7:13+
The virgin shall be with child...Emmanuel

Is 9:6+
A [Davidic] child is given us...his names

Is 11
The Shoot shall sprout...his gifts

Is 40
The Book of Consolation

Is 32
Kingdom of justice,... peace

Is 42, 49, 50, 52-53
The Servant of the Lord

Is 55
Come, you who are thirsty. My word does not come back to me empty

Is 59-50
The hand of the Lord is not too short to save

Is 63-4
Beautiful prayer

Is 65-66
The new world

Jeremiah

Jer 1:1-19
JEREMIAH'S CALL

Jer 2:13
Broken cisterns, that hold no water

Jer 5:21
Eyes, but see not; ears but hear not

Jer 7:31
Valley of Ben-Hinnom—idols

Jer 8:22
   No balm in Gilead

Jer 9:23
   Let not the wise man glory in his wisdom....

Jer 12:1-4; 15:15-18; 17:14-18; 18:19-23; 20:7-18
   THE CONFESSIONS

Jer 13:23
   The Ethiopian...the leopard

Jer 23:5
   A righteous shoot to David

Jer 23:29
   Is not my word like fire...like a hammer shattering rocks

Jer 25:11
   Seventy years...in exile

Jer 31:22
   The woman must encompass the man

Jer 31:31-34
   The New Covenant; I will place my law within hearts

Jer 36
   Burning the message

Jer 38
   Night in a cistern

Ezekiel

Ezek 1:1+
   Inaugural vision; God's hand was upon me

Ezek 15:1-9
Parable of the vine

Ezek 17:22
A tender shoot....

Ezek 18:1+
Personal responsibility (also 33:10-21)

Ezek 34:1+
Shepherds, bad and good

Ezek 36:1+
Regeneration—new heart and spirit

Ezek 37:1+
Vision of the dry bones

Ezek 40-48
The new Israel

Ezek 47:1+
The wonderful stream—*vidi aquam*

Daniel

Dan 2:31
Statue with feet of clay

Dan 5:1+
Handwriting on the wall

Dan 6:1+
Daniel in the lion's den

Dan 7:1+
Four beasts from the sea

Dan 9:1-27
  The 70 weeks

Dan 12:1-4
  Future glory

Dan 13:1+
  Susanna saved

Hosea

Hos 4:1-2, 6
  People perishing for want of knowledge

Hos 4:13
  The high-places

Hos 6:4 12:3
  Piety...like a morning cloud

Hos 8:7
  Sow the wind, reap the whirlwind

Hos 11:1+
  Tenderness of God

Joel

Joel 1:4+
  The locusts

Joel 2:13
  Rend your hearts, not your garments

Joel 3:1+
  I will pour out my spirit

Joel 3:9
Get ready for contention

Joel 3:2, 12
The valley of decision

Amos

Amos 1 and 2
I will not revoke my word

Amos 4
Yet you returned not to me

Amos 4:12
Prepare to meet your God, O Israel

Amos 5:6, 14
Seek me...seek good and not evil

Amos 5:18, 20
The Day of the Lord

Amos 5:21
I hate, I spurn your feasts, your solemnities. If you would offer me holocausts, then let justice surge like water, and goodness like an unfailing stream

Am 8:11
I will send famine upon the land: not a famine of bread, or thirst for water, but for hearing the word of the Lord

Amos 9:13
The days are coming...when harvest will follow directly after plowing, the treading of grapes soon after sowing, the mountains run with new wine and the hills all flow with it

Micah

Mic 2:1+
   Greed for land

Mic 2:12
   The remnant of Israel, the Lord at their head

Mic 4:4
   Every man shall sit under his own vine, or under his own fig tree, undisturbed

Mic 5:2
   From you (Bethlehem) shall come one who is to be ruler in Israel, whose origin is from of old, from ancient times

Mic 5:7
   The remnant of Jacob

Mic 5:13
   Sacred poles...Baal, Asherah, pagan gods

Mic 6:8
   What the Lord requires of you: only do what is right, love goodness, and walk humbly with your God

Mic 7:19
   Cast into the depths of the sea all our sins

Zephaniah

Zeph 1:15
   Near is the day of the Lord...the great day A day of wrath is that day...of anguish and distress, a day of darkness and gloom, a day of thick, black clouds

Zeph 2:3+
Seek the Lord, all you humble of the earth, seek justice, seek humility. Perhaps you may be sheltered on the day of the Lord's anger

Zeph 3:12
I will leave as a remnant in your midst, a people humble and lowly

Zechariah

Zech 11:13
My wages...thirty pieces of silver

Zech 12:10
They shall look on him whom they have thrust through and they shall mourn for him as for an only son

Malachi

Mal 1:11
From the rising of the sun to its setting, my name is great among the nations

Mal 2:7
The lips of the priest are to keep knowledge. Instruction is to be sought from his mouth, for he is the messenger of the Lord of hosts

7. A List of Messianic Texts

Genesis 3:15
The seed of the Woman

Genesis 49:10-11
The scepter...Judah

Numbers 24:17
A star...from Jacob

2 Samuel 7:12, 15
David's heir

Amos 5:15, 18
The remnant—the Day

Amos 9:11-15
Messianic joy

Isaiah 7:14
The virgin...Emmanuel

Isaiah 9:2
A great light

Isaiah 9:6-7
The child—Davidic, authority, power, forever

Isaiah 11:1-9
Spiritual gifts

Isaiah 42:1-9
The Servant of the Lord

Isaiah 49:1-6
The Servant of the Lord

Isaiah 50:4-11
The Servant of the Lord

Isaiah 52:13+
The Servant of the Lord

Micah 5:1-4
Bethlehem

Jeremiah 31:31-34
The New Covenant

Zephaniah 1:15
The Day of the Lord

Zephaniah 3:12+
The remnant

Habakkuk 3:17+
Problem of evil—trust in God

Ezekiel 18:1-32
Personal responsibility

Ezekiel 33:10-20
Individual retribution

Ezekiel 34:11-23
The Good Shepherd

Ezekiel 37:1+
Vision of the dry bones

Ezekiel 40-48
The new theocracy

Daniel 9:20+
The 70 weeks

Haggai 2:23
Zerubbabel, signet ring

Zechariah 3:8
The Branch (Shoot)

Zechariah 9:9
Messianic restoration

Malachi 1:11
A clean oblation

Joel 2:28-32
Promise of the Spirit

St. Paul Book & Media Centers

ALASKA
750 West 5th Ave., Anchorage, AK 99501; 907-272-8183

CALIFORNIA
3908 Sepulveda Blvd., Culver City, CA 90230; 310-397-8676
5945 Balboa Ave., San Diego, CA 92111; 619-565-9181
46 Geary Street, San Francisco, CA 94108; 415-781-5180

FLORIDA
145 S.W. 107th Ave., Miami, FL 33174; 305-559-6715

HAWAII
1143 Bishop Street, Honolulu, HI 96813; 808-521-2731

ILLINOIS
172 North Michigan Ave., Chicago, IL 60601; 312-346-4228

LOUISIANA
4403 Veterans Memorial Blvd., Metairie, LA 70006; 504-887-7631

MASSACHUSETTS
50 St. Paul's Ave., Jamaica Plain, Boston, MA 02130; 617-522-8911
Rte. 1, 885 Providence Hwy., Dedham, MA 02026; 617-326-5385

MISSOURI
9804 Watson Rd., St. Louis, MO 63126; 314-965-3512

NEW JERSEY
561 U.S. Route 1, Wick Plaza, Edison, NJ 08817; 908-572-1200

NEW YORK
150 East 52nd Street, New York, NY 10022; 212-754-1110
78 Fort Place, Staten Island, NY 10301; 718-447-5071

OHIO
2105 Ontario Street, Cleveland, OH 44115; 216-621-9427

PENNSYLVANIA
Northeast Shopping Center, 9171-A Roosevelt Blvd. (between Grant Ave.
& Welsh Rd.), Philadelphia, PA 19114; 610-277-7728

SOUTH CAROLINA
243 King Street, Charleston, SC 29401; 803-577-0175

TENNESSEE
4811 Poplar Ave., Memphis, TN 38117; 901-761-2987

TEXAS
114 Main Plaza, San Antonio, TX 78205; 210-224-8101

VIRGINIA
1025 King Street, Alexandria, VA 22314; 703-549-3806

GUAM
285 Farenholt Ave., Suite 308, Tamuning, Guam 96911; 671-649-4377

CANADA
3022 Dufferin Street, Toronto, Ontario, Canada M6B 3T5; 416-781-9131